Victory Outreach Ministries International

and

Founders Sonny and Julie Arguinzoni

Present this limited edition

of

TREASURES OUT OF DARKNESS

This Book is Number

————————————

of Ten Thousand.

Treasures Out of Darkness

by
Sonny and Julie Arguinzoni

FIRST EDITION
1991

Cover design: Rob Kerby
Library of Congress Catalog Number: 91-062440
ISBN: 0-89221-214-4

If you are interested in knowing more about the ministry of Victory World Outreach International, write to:
Sonny & Julie Arguinzoni
P.O. Box 2828
La Puente, CA 91746

CONTENTS

Acknowledgments

Special thanks to the following who have given countless hours of unselfish labor and love in preparation of this manuscript:

Joesy and Steve Pineda

Charlie and Evelyn "Pogie" Moreno

Kathy Clark and the Victory Outreach office staff

This book woult not have been possible without the countless "Treasures" whose response to the message of the gospel caused it to be carried to the four corners of the earth.

Dedication

To our beautiful children who endured years of hardship as the unfolding of the vision to reach treasures out of darkness became a reality:

Deborah — *Our firstborn*
> For giving up your "little place" so that others could have a new chance at life.

Doreen —
> For the many times you desired to have friends over and live "normal" and we had to regretfully say "no."

Sonny Junior —
> For all the "time" you allowed us to give to others although rightfully yours ... you never complained.

Georgina —
> For willingly "sharing" your home and your mom and dad so that others could be saved.

Foreword

What a joy to read this incredible story!

Here is the real-life adventure of humble people willing to let Jesus Christ rule their lives. The result is that our mighty God has taken a dead-end heroin addict off of the bloody streets of New York City and has used him to evangelize in the great cities of the world.

I do not exaggerate! Because of the selfless obedience of Sonny Arguinzoni, great revival is taking place in the concrete jungles of Los Angeles! Throughout the United States, Mexico, Europe, and even Africa, converts today are being nurtured in a lifestyle of righteousness, holiness, and evangelism!

This will be the new generation — sold-out Christians willing to sacrifice everything, ready to turn their homes into Holy Ghost hospitals, and prepared to turn their entire lives over to Jesus! They are warriors — throwing back Satan's darkness and snatching the damned out of the jaws of hell!

None of them are superstars, but that's where today's Church is headed, my friend! Soon, it will be just us little guys, you and me, hundreds of thousands of Christians working one-on-one, joyously winning one soul at a time to Jesus.

I am so gratified to be able to call Sonny Arguinzoni my spiritual son! Just as I was young evangelist David Wilkerson's first gang leader to come to the Lord, Sonny was my first Timothy. He was the first heroin addict to turn everything over to Jesus back during my early years of preaching on the streets.

Now, when I go preaching and witnessing with him, I gaze out at the thousands that his ministry has led to the Lord and I weep with inner joy. Do I dare call them my spiritual grandkids and great-grandkids? They were brought to Jesus by my Timothy and by the hundreds that he has brought into ministry! My heart burns with excitement as I know that I was permitted by God to have a founding role in this incredible ministry.

As you read this book, I pray that you will be inspired to new boldness and a yearning to evangelize.

Fantastic things are happening.

You can be a part of it.

Come, catch the vision!

Nicky Cruz
1991

Chapter One

JULIE

"The food's on the table. Everyone come right now or it will get cold," Mom called from the kitchen. She didn't have to call twice. We were all hungry and rushed to the table and sat down. Even Dad was there visiting.

"Gary," Mom yelled, "get in here right now! Gary, did you hear me? Julie, where's your brother?"

"Mom, he's in the bathroom and he's been in there quite awhile." My brother Gary was addicted to heroin and my mom and dad were trying everything to help him, but nothing seemed to be working.

Dad rushed from the table, ran to the bathroom, began pounding on the door, and yelled, "Gary, Gary, open the door," but there was only silence. Dad slammed his body against the door, breaking it open. "Oh, my God, Gary's over-dosed. Call the paramedics!"

There they were in plain sight for all of us to see: a spoon, needle, and powder...Gary was fixing in the bathroom. Dad and my older brother Jimmy carried his lifeless body into the living room. His face was turning blue. All of us were crying and screaming. Just then, Gary started gurgling and Mother screamed, "That's the death rattle! Oh, my God, do something. Do something! Gary's dying."

I don't know why, but Mom ran to the phone and called her sister, crying into the phone, "Lecia, pray for Gary, he's O.D.'d."

Then she handed the phone to my dad and he made the emergency call.

Jimmy and I began giving Gary artificial respiration, but our attempts were futile, he didn't respond. When the paramedics got there they declared him dead. "It's too late, he's gone," one of them said.

They retook all his vital signs. Downcast, one of the paramedics again said, "We're too late, he's gone."

My mother went crazy, she was running around the house screaming and crying, "What did I do wrong? What's happening? Help him, help him, do something!"

Dad had also lost it. It broke my heart to see my father crying, he sobbed like a baby. In the midst of all this, my Aunt Lecia called back. I ran to the phone, and picked it up. She said, "Julie, I have been praying and I want you to tell your mother that Gary's going to be okay."

"Aunt Lecia, it's too late, Gary's dead," I sobbed.

"Julie, Julie, are you still there?" my aunt asked.

"Yes, I'm still here," I responded.

"Gary's going to be all right. You will see. God told me!"

"Sure, Aunt Lecia, sure," I said, thinking that she was a little strange, as I looked at Gary's lifeless body lying on the floor.

The paramedics were already sitting down. It was horrible. A sick feeling overtook me, watching my brother die like that.

How can this be? We are a good middle class family, I thought. My thoughts drifted to how we got ourselves in this situation.

I have three brothers and two sisters. I was raised in East Los Angeles, where my parents owned a grocery store. I had worked in the store since I was old enough to be of value. I was used to working real hard, and would get up early and get everything ready for the store to open. My mom and dad seemed to have a beautiful marriage. We grew up going on vacations together and were real happy. I had a wonderful childhood.

I always had a lot of love for my father and we had a very close relationship. I kind of idolized my dad. I thought he was the tallest, most handsome man that I had ever met. It wasn't until I got older that I realized that he was not really tall, he's short! However, he was real good to me. When I was eight years old I remember he'd get side jobs painting houses so he'd have to leave early in the morning. I'd get up with him, press his overalls, and fix his lunch. I loved those special moments with my dad, I'd always put little surprises in his lunch, like bubble gum and candy.

When I was fifteen we found out that my dad was having an affair with another woman, and that broke up the family. One Christmas Eve I saw him with her and he didn't know that I had seen them. I went home and told my mom what I had seen. My mother was already aware that there were some problems, but because I had seen them, that was the last straw, and they ended up getting divorced. My mom and I kept the store and ran it by ourselves after that.

It was real difficult during that time because my brother Gary started getting into drugs and my older brother became an alcoholic.

The first time that I found out that Gary was using heroin I felt so ashamed, because I had always felt my family was something to be proud of. Now my brother was an addict and that simply wasn't acceptable in our social circles.

My mother and dad started searching for a solution even though they were divorced.

My Aunt Lecia was a very powerful Christian, and my mother's father had been a pastor, but my mother had turned away from the things of God when she was twelve years old. As a family we never went to church or read the Bible, we were raised without God.

Sobbing, I slowly hung up the phone in total hope-lessness and despair. "Mom, you will never believe what Aunt Lecia sa...."

Suddenly, Gary bounced straight up like a spring, as though someone had taken hold of his hand and pulled him up.

"What's going on, Man?" Gary asked.

His mind was instantly clear and he appeared to be totally drug free! The paramedics rushed over to him, laid him back down, and began taking his vital signs. "I can't believe it," one of them said, "but everything checks out perfect."

None of us could believe our eyes, nor could the paramedics. Mom began jumping up and down, shouting, "I've seen a miracle. I've seen a miracle! Thank You, God! Thank You, Jesus! There is a God, a real God! My son is alive, and it's a miracle. Lecia did hear from God!"

Everything suddenly changed, we were ecstatic with joy. We started hugging and kissing Gary. He didn't quite know what to make of all the commotion. After the paramedics left, the police who came with them said to Gary, "We're sorry, Son, but you are under arrest for possession. We have to take you in." Our joy in his miraculous healing was short-lived...this was Gary's first arrest. I looked at my mother and saw the agony and heartache in her eyes.

After dinner I tried to recall everything that had

happened. In my heart I knew somehow that God was in all of this and Gary was alive because God had answered Aunt Lecia's prayers. God showed us something that day, but we didn't realize it. Nobody came to explain anything to us or we would have been ready right then to receive Christ Jesus. That day, I saw God's power for the very first time in my life.

Even though they were divorced, Mom and Dad lived together while Gary was in prison. It broke my heart to see them struggle for an answer to their problems, when there wasn't one. Night after night, I would go to sleep hearing my mother cry.

"Julie," my dad said, "I want you to live with your sister during your senior year. (Although we had never told our parents, my sister's husband was also a heroin addict.) I feel that your mother and I must move up north for Gary's sake before he gets out of jail and returns to this neighborhood."

The following week my parents moved 400 miles away. The move didn't help Gary one bit. As a matter of fact, they moved next door to a drug dealer. Life for them in northern California got worse, and several months later they returned to El Monte, which is about twenty miles from East L.A. I was glad to see them.

Our new next door neighbor was a Christian, and often testified to my mom. He said to her, "I was a drug addict, but I found Jesus and He was my answer. Why don't you come to my church and discover the truth?"

By then my cousins were also inviting us to go to their church, so we went. I had only been to church on special holidays, so I was somewhat apprehensive about the whole thing. The music was something else. It was beautiful and soothing to me, I felt peace within.

When the preacher started talking he told us, "Jesus Christ said, 'I am the resurrection and the life. He who believes in me will live, even though he dies; and whoever lives and believes in me will never die'" (John 11:25, 26; NIV).

Wow, that's something! I thought. *The minister talks just like Jesus is alive.* Step by step he explained the gospel to the congregation. However, I thought it was just for me.

He said, "Jesus Christ, the Son of God, died on Calvary. He shed His blood so that you could be cleansed of all sin. Without the shedding of the Blood, there is no remission of sin."

I turned to my cousin and said in a whisper, "You mean if I ask Jesus to forgive my sins and I believe that he died on the Cross and was resurrected for me, I'll be saved?"

"Yes," he replied. "Julie, Jesus shed His blood on Calvary for you. You can know today that your sins are forgiven and that you will go to heaven when you die. Just ask Jesus to come into your heart and believe."

I turned and continued to listen to the preacher. My heart was pounding and it all sounded so beautiful. If only it was that easy, "just believe."

When the preacher said, "If you would like to accept Jesus as your personal Saviour, come forward and we'll pray for you."

I thought, *This is the most beautiful thing I have ever heard!* Nothing could keep me from the altar. Jesus was what I was looking for. I almost ran to the altar. I prayed and cried, and asked Jesus to come into my heart and be my Saviour. Within a week my entire family accepted Christ. We found a place to go every night and hear about Jesus. The whole family was going every night, crying and praying. This went on for days.

One morning as I was getting ready to go to school, I was listening to the radio. By now we had been going to church for about a month. The radio preacher asked, "Are you saved?" I didn't know if I was saved yet, or not. I didn't understand what he meant when he said, "Just believe." It just didn't penetrate, salvation couldn't be that simple. I thought you had to do something special — not just believe. I was in turmoil because I didn't know if I was saved or not. He kept asking, "Are you saved?"

I would say, "I don't know."

Then the radio preacher asked, "Do you feel like going to a dance?"

"No, I don't feel like doing that," I responded to the radio.

"Do you feel like drinking?"

I said, "No, I don't feel like drinking."

"Do you feel like smoking?"

I did smoke, but I said, "No, I don't feel like smoking."

Then the radio preacher asked, "Do you believe Jesus shed His blood on Calvary for you?"

"Yes, I believe that," I responded to the radio.

"Have you asked Him to forgive your sins?"

I said, "Yes, I have done that."

"Do you believe He has forgiven you?"

I said, "Yes, I believe He has."

"Do you feel like praising God?"

"Yes, I feel like praising God!" I almost shouted.

Then he asked, "Do you feel like going to church, and praying?" He then started describing all those things that I felt like doing.

"Yes! That's the way! That's the way I feel and want to be!" I responded.

"Then," he said, "you are SAVED!"

I started shouting, laughing, and crying, "I'm saved! I'm really saved!" Everything had changed, but I hadn't realized what God had done in my life. I was a new creature in Christ!

I went into the kitchen and told my mom, "Mom, Mom, I'm saved! I'm saved!"

At that point I realized that I was saved, Christ had really changed my life, and had come into my heart when I asked Him to a month earlier.

I went back to school and all my friends were amazed at what God had done in my life. I started witnessing at school. My boyfriend, at the time, got saved. It wasn't long until a lot of my friends also accepted Jesus.

Chapter Two

THE JUNKIE

"Sonny, get out of that bed and get ready for church," my mom yelled from the hallway. I had decided the night before that I was never going to go to that dull church again. I was twelve and too old and tough to have anything to do with God. Who needed Him? Not me! I had better things to do.

"You guys go on without me. I don't want to go to church no more." They fussed a little more at me but they let me stay home. From that day on, my days of attending church with my parents were over.

I was raised in a Christian home. My parents lived a very legalistic life and actually turned me off to Christianity and the church. All I heard was, "You can't do this, you can't do that." Everything was sin, especially to my father, who was very strict.

Dad was very much involved in the church where he was a deacon and was well-respected. He was very consistent in his attendance, and headed up the Sunday school. I had to attend because they made me, until I rebelled. It wasn't long until I started running around with the kids of the neighborhood.

One day one of the guys pulled out a joint of marijuana, and I tried it. Suddenly, I felt like I was really alive and could take on anyone. Man, I was a new breed of Superman! I liked it, so I started using it pretty often. I was drinking wine already, so taking a stick of pot was no problem. In a short time I started taking what they called goofballs, which were like barbiturates. They would give me a real high.

Most of the guys I hung around with were twelve or thirteen years old. Our gang would only take coke, marijuana, or a few pills.

My adventure with cops and jail began even before I started using heroin. Even at thirteen I soon found out that pills and coke cost money, so I thought the easiest and coolest thing to do was to steal cars. I wouldn't get much, maybe only three hundred to five hundred bucks, depending on the car.

Then a couple of my friends began to run with another gang and experimented with heroin. When they came back I realized they looked strange, and were on a different high. They said to me, "Sonny, we've tried snorting heroin and you can't believe what it does for us. Man, you've got to try it." I went out with them and took a snort. I got really sick. They told me, "Sonny, that's natural, the next time you're gonna feel better." I didn't take it again for a while, then I thought I'd try it just one more time. I started snorting it, and man, it did its thing. I was on my way at thirteen.

Sonny with the gang.

The guys from Brooklyn in my neighborhood would hang around together, and sometimes we would fight the guys from the lower East Side of Manhattan. We had our own little territory and fought different gangs, went to dances, and sometimes got into fights there. When I started using heroin, I totally got away from those guys. *That was kid's stuff,* I thought. I got into a more "with-it" crowd, and they were all older guys, eighteen to twenty.

I was just fifteen when I began to take what you call

skin pops. Instead of snorting it I had somebody shoot me on the surface of the skin with the needle. I really began to like it and soon developed a daily habit.

About a year later, one of the guys came up to me and said, "Sonny, you are really wasting the stuff. Don't skin pop it, man, shoot it right into your veins."

"You're crazy, Man. Into my veins?" I responded.

"Sure, here I'll show you how it's done," and he mainlined it into my vein.

The sudden rush was awesome! Wow, in an instant I was gone, it was a high like I had never had before.

At first my junkie buddies had to inject me in the vein, because I didn't know how to do it. But eventually I learned how to inject myself. I still wasn't really hooked. I would take it for three days and then I would stop for a week, and then take it again, and stop. Eventually, that led me to taking it every day. I was hooked.

Getting the money for a fix possessed me twenty-four hours a day. I would steal anything in sight, but stealing cars became real easy and I got hooked on stealing them.

One night I saw this beautiful blue Cadillac and the steal was easy. It was so beautiful I decided to pick up some of the guys and go cruising before I turned it in to the fence.

"Hey, guys, hop in," I said. "This is really posh. Let's go cruising for an hour or so."

"Sonny, this is real neat. How fast can it go?"

At the age of fifteen, that was a challenge no one could resist, so I floored the gas pedal, and away we went high and flying.

Suddenly, there were sounds of screeching tires, and something that sounded like bombs going off. Then it all stopped. Silence.

When I came to, there was glass and blood everywhere. In pain, I slowly turned around and saw Duke and Frankie. They were covered with blood and deadly quiet. I shook them, yelling, "Wake up! Wake up! Hey man, we've got to get out of here before the cops come! Let's go!"

I knew they were dead because blood was slowly oozing out of Duke's forehead. Oh my God, I thought, *they are really dead! I gotta split.* I slowly crawled out the window and headed for home and tried to clean myself up. I was cut up a little and bruised a lot. I felt terrible that I had killed a couple of my buddies.

Mom called from the bedroom, "Sonny, is that you? Are you all right?"

"Sure, Mom," I responded. "I'm okay. I'm just a little dizzy. I think I'll lie down for a while." I had a wash cloth over the cut on my forehead, so Mom couldn't see it and went to bed. At that moment, I needed rest and sleep.

I got in bed and pulled the covers over me, I was in total darkness. I felt the blood still oozing from my cut, but sleep was coming fast and it felt so good. I was relaxing, until suddenly, I heard banging on the front door. My heart started pounding and my face flushed — I knew who it was! My guts told me it was the cops.

I heard them ask Mom, "Does Sonny Arguinzoni live here?" I wanted to run, but I couldn't. As a matter of fact, I was so weak that I could hardly move.

Mom pulled back the covers and there stood two cops looking straight into my eyes. Mom let out a scream and said, "Oh, dear Jesus, Sonny!"

Mom stood there with that hurt look in her eyes.

The policemen said, "This boy is covered with blood. He's in bad shape, we have to get him to the hospital. Get the first-aid box, we have got to stop the bleeding or this boy will die in his bed. Son, we'll talk to you later concerning a stolen Cadillac and an accident."

As we were going out the door, I looked at Mom and saw her anguish, frustration, and deep, deep hurt. *But that's her problem*, I thought, *I'm going to be booked for murder, they just aren't telling me.*

As they were fixing me up at the hospital's emergency room, I was soon aware of two very familiar voices. I recognized them — it was Duke and Frankie! They were alive!

As soon as I was bandaged, I was taken to the police station for booking. When we got there, I couldn't believe it, but there stood Frankie and Duke. Our eyes met and we said nothing. They had ratted on me!

Frankie had told them I had stolen the car and was driving.

I was booked and sentenced to six months.

When I walked out of the court room I acted real tough. The stories I had heard about what happens to fifteen-year-olds **really** had me terrified.

As the guard took me to my cell, the sight was awesome and there was steel everywhere. We were walking on a cat-walk, three stories high. The doors to the cells were solid except for a small slot where the guards could look in or the prisoner could look out. The guys in the cells were looking at us and yelling, "What ya in for?" "Hey kid, got a smoke?" "Hey, he's a young one!"

Slowly the guard opened the door. The cell was real small and dingy. When the door slammed shut behind me, I could hear the echoes reverberate down through the halls. I was alone with my thoughts. *What's going on? How will Mom ever handle this?* I had lost all my freedom. The night was dark, long, and frightening.

The next morning, walking to the mess hall, I didn't think my legs would carry me at the thought of what might happen to me. When I walked in, I noticed some of the older guys from the neighborhood were there. "Hey Sonny, come on over here," one of them yelled at me. "What are you in for? Possession?"

"Yeah," I answered.

"Hey Man, don't you worry about nothin' Sonny — us

guys are gonna see that no one messes with you or they'll answer to us!"

They all knew me and were already well-established within the prison. I came from a well-known notorious neighborhood in Brooklyn. With those guys behind me no one dared touch me.

I wasn't there very long the first time because they changed my crime from a felony to a misdemeanor and let me out early.

Soon after that, I turned the ripe old age of sixteen, and was arrested again. This time, it was for possession and using heroin and marijuana. In New York, at the time, if you got caught for possession all you would get was six months. When I stood before the judge for sentencing, I wasn't really worried.

"Sonny Arguinzoni," the judge began, "this court sentences you to six months. However, it is obvious to this court that you are addicted to heroin. If you choose, I will permit you to go to the Lexington, Kentucky Drug Treatment Facility for the cure."

Of course I chose to go to Lexington and went through the whole program. While I was in Lexington, there were also some guys there that I knew. When I got out, another guy came out with me who was from the lower East Side. When we arrived back in New York, the first place we headed for was a connection's house, and bought a fix. Physically I was fine, but mentally I was still a drug addict, and knew it.

Man, I couldn't wait to get that needle in my vein. Shooting up after I'd been dry for a while gave me a real beautiful, wonderful high.

The next thing on my agenda was getting money, and I would need lots of it. I would almost have to steal a car every other day. But, I needed some money now. I thought maybe Mom or Dad had bought a new radio or something while I was locked up. I could hock that for what I needed that day.

I'd forgotten all about it being Saturday when both Mom and Dad would be home from work, so I was a little surprised when I walked into the living room and there was Dad with his stocking feet propped up on the sofa, reading. I had been gone for six months and casually said, "Hi, Dad. I'm home." I knew he wouldn't be glad to see me, not like I was then.

He looked me over, and I could see from the hurt look in his eyes that he could tell I was loaded.

The bedroom door was closed, but I could hear Mom's voice in there, rising and sinking, rising and sinking. I shifted my weight uneasily from one foot to the other. I knew she was praying because prayer always made me want to get as far away from the house as possible. I could feel it bugging me now, even when I was pretty loaded and was supposed to feel so good that nothing could bother me, yet I was very uncomfortable.

"So you're home." Dad's eyes were fixed on mine. Slowly he put his feet on the floor and stood to face me.

I was almost a head taller than he, but suddenly he looked forbidding.

"You can turn right around and march out the door!" He pointed toward the open door to the hallway. "This isn't your home anymore." His mouth was twitching, as if he wanted to cry. I just stood there, staring.

"What's going on?" I looked at him. "I'm just coming home and you're sending me out on the street — your own son?" I shouldn't have said it. Already I could tell he was fighting to hold back the tears.

"My own son!" His voice rose. "My son who steals every penny from his mother's purse; my son who took my last suit to the pawnshop; my son who brings junkies home to shoot heroin in our bathroom; my son who doesn't care about his mother's tears?" My father was shouting now, but I really didn't care because I was feeling free and easy all over and just wanted to go somewhere and doze off for a while.

The door to the bedroom opened and there was my mother in the doorway. I blinked in amazement. Her face was streaked with tears but she was smiling, looking as serene as if she didn't have a care in the world. Somehow it bugged me.

Mother walked steadily over to where Dad was standing and put her hand on his arm, patting it reassuringly.

"Don't worry about Sonny, Papa," she said softly. "God just told me he's gonna be all right."

Dad shook her hand off and threw his arms up in a gesture of despair. "My God, Mama!" he exclaimed. "Sonny is getting worse every day! What do you mean he's gonna be all right?"

My mom smiled again, though her eyes were still gleaming with tears. She had to swallow before she spoke.

"I don't care if he's getting worse. God told me he's gonna be all right." Her cheerful confidence was a puzzle to me.

My dad shook his head. "He can't stay around here anymore; he's gonna have to leave." I could tell there would be no talking him out of that decision. Mom didn't even try.

After that, Mom and Dad wouldn't let me stay at home. I lived wherever I could find a place to put my head.

The drug scene is an environment of survival. You have to go out and get the money, and then try to survive within that asphalt jungle. There are people burning and robbing each other. Then there are the girls. Type one is the "friend." They are friends of yours, and you actually fix together. There is seldom any desire to have sex with them because they are like one of the boys. You would send them out to sell their bodies and they'd come back with the money so you could fix together.

"Type two" were girlfriends who were not involved in

drugs. Usually, I didn't like girls that were involved in drugs.

But that wasn't always the case. After I had the run-in with my dad, I headed straight for a bar where I knew Rosie would be waiting.

Sure enough, Rosie was there, her flaming red hair easy to spot in the crowd.

"Sonny!" Her face lit up, and she threw her arms around me. "It's good to see you!" She nuzzled close and we inched our way around the crowded dance floor, swaying to the music from the jukebox. I closed my eyes and tried to get back into that good high feeling again, but Mom's words were swirling through my head. Strange, they bugged me more than Dad's ordering me out. What could she mean — that I'd be all right?

I looked down at Rosie and suddenly noticed something I'd never seen before — her red hair was streaked and black at the roots, and caked with gummy layers of hairspray. I must have drawn back, because Rosie looked up and laughed loudly.

"Getting edgy, Sonny boy?" She pressed her body closer to mine. "You've been locked up in prison too long!"

I'd never noticed how thick and dead her makeup was. It didn't hide the dark lines around her eyes or the sagging at her mouth. She'd lost a couple of teeth and the black spaces made her look repulsive to me. Her voice had a shrill tone and I could smell that she hadn't had a bath for a long time. The strong, cheap perfume only made it worse.

I looked over her head, and the air in the bar was foul with the stench of bodies, liquor, and smoke. Everybody was making a lot of noise, like they were having a good time, but suddenly I could see they were sick, sick inside.

"Man," I mumbled, "I gotta get out of here!" I made my way to the washroom where I'd stashed my outfit and a bag of heroin under the sink. My hands shook while I prepared the fix and got ready to shoot up. As soon as the heroin hit my bloodstream, I could feel my head clear up and get light and peaceful. I hurried back to Rosie, and somehow she looked young and pretty to me again.

In a few weeks I was arrested again. This time I did six months behind bars and was released. Then I got arrested again, and I did another six months. So my life went into a downward spiral, in and out, in and out of jail. All I ever got was actually six months at a time. I got used to it and as soon as I got arrested I waived my rights, and I went back to jail. I would go in and I knew exactly when I was getting out with good behavior. It would be four months and fifteen days. I got to the point where I was pulling armed robberies. I didn't get caught for those things or I would have done a lot of time.

I became a slave to the drugs and I couldn't change,

no matter how much I tried. Every time I got out of jail I would promise that this time I would stop. And I would last maybe two weeks. Then eventually I would miss the environment. I felt alone and needed someone to hang around with because I missed the action of the drug scene. I would come back just to see them, and say to myself, *I'm gonna be strong, I'm not gonna use, I'm just gonna see how they're doing.* I would come by a few times, see them, then leave again.

The scene on the streets was all action. It was a mad rush and it was as addictive as the heroin that I put in my veins — it was the city's "Call of the Wild." It was the same rush and thrill of sky diving, race car driving, fire eating, mountain climbing, or Russian Roulette. It was death-defying and pure excitement. Girls, drugs, cops, stealing, running — all added up to one "happy day!" I couldn't stand being away from it.

The guys I ran with were real rough and tough. We controlled most of the drugs in the neighborhood. Because of our heroin habit we would go in and pull an armed robbery. All of us carried weapons. Knives, guns, and what have you. Many of the guys had their faces cut because of fights. Many times we used to take the drugs away from the connection, from the dealer. Also we would go to another neighborhood and find the person who was dealing drugs, pull a gun on him, and take his heroin away.

I lived on the cutting edge. It was like I could die any

day. My mom and dad knew it, and they even got insurance on me. Dad would say, "You're not gonna live too long. You're gonna die." Many of my friends were dying on the rooftops from overdoses. We stashed our paraphernalia on the rooftops of apartment buildings. That way we could all shoot up at the same time. Some guys would actually die from overdoses and we would have to leave them there and just walk away. It was the type of environment that I was living in.

You couldn't trust anybody. I mean, you had to watch out because you had the rats, the guys who were informers. You could be hanging around with an informer who was working for the police. He most likely had been arrested so he would make a deal with them, and turn you in. I was always watching my back. I never knew when I was going to walk into a set-up. I thrived on that because it was exciting. Having the police chasing us gave me a real rush.

I didn't know how to hold a job and never had one for more than six months. I didn't have any trade. I was an eighth grade drop-out. There was nothing that I could do to make my money except wheeling and dealing on the streets.

The first time I broke into a house was a real trauma. A couple of guys went with me. We had it all figured out — two of us would do the stealing and one would be the lookout.

We walked up to the door and rang the bell. We also

knocked real hard. When no one answered, I took the screwdriver out of my pocket and slowly pried the door open. As I slowly opened the door, my heart was beating so hard and fast, I just knew that if there was anyone in the house that "beating" would give us away.

"Ray," I whispered. "You take the living room and I'll get the bedrooms. Hurry up! We don't want to get caught."

I then slowly walked back to the bedroom. When I turned the knob and began to open the door, it squeaked. I broke out in a cold sweat and thought I would faint with fear. I grabbed the loose bills and change, the jewelry that looked expensive, and a transistor radio. There wasn't much in there.

I got to the hall as Ray was coming out of the living room. "What did you get?" I asked.

"Man, a real good stereo and this portable TV," Ray responded.

"Let's get out of here!"

We took the stuff to the fence and got $100 — enough for each of us to be okay for a day. Then we had to have more money. We took money from anybody and if the person spoke up we would stab them, beat them up, and leave them lying on the ground. We had to have money for drugs — at any cost!

The fix would last, depending how hooked you were, for five or six hours. After that you would be okay for awhile, but that evening you would have to have another fix or you couldn't make it. Twelve hours was the outer limit.

One day while walking the streets, stoned almost out of my mind, I noticed that a tall, skinny, square-looking guy was in my neighborhood. He walked up to me and said, "Hi, my name is David Wilkerson. I've come all the way from Pennsylvania to let you know that God loves you and wants to come into your life."

I told him, "Get lost, you are in the wrong place, Man. I'm clean. Just leave me alone. I don't want anything to do with you."

I knew he didn't belong in the neighborhood and assumed he was a cop.

For days and weeks ahead this guy really bugged us with all his talk about Jesus and what this Jesus could do for us. To him, Jesus was the answer to every need a person had or would ever have.

"Watch what you say around this guy. He is either a 'holy nut' or a Narc," I told the other guys. "Yeah, Man, we feel the same way," they responded.

"I have never met anyone like him. He seems really hooked on this Jesus," I said.

I was standing against a building and there he was again. There was no way I could avoid him. "Son, why don't you let me take you home with me and let you kick the habit. I really want to help you. My name is David Wilkerson," he said.

I thought to myself, I n*eed a place to stay tonight,*

what have I got to lose? Maybe I can steel a TV or a stereo from him.

He insisted we go by the folks' house to tell them what was going on. My Mom just glowed at the thought of me going home with a preacher.

His home was on Staten Island and I spent the night there. He read the Bible to me and said a prayer over me. That made me feel good.

The next day, I was riding in his car and was really sick, needing a fix. I looked at him and said, "Preacher, I know you mean good, but you don't understand. I have a drug habit and right now I'm sick and I need a fix." Then I just threw the door open of his car, and I ran out yelling, "I'm sorry, but I just can't make it!"

"Sonny, I'd rather you were dead than return to drugs!" David yelled at me, his "one-day convert."

Who's he kidding. I am hooked and will be for the rest of my life. I'm a junkie. This guy doesn't know the score, I thought. I ran hard, hoping I'd never see him again.

I was buying heroin and cutting it with milk sugar to resell. My habit, that was costing $75 a day then, would be $500 in today's figures. I decided that if I was lucky, I could last another few years on the street, and that would be the end of it.

I saw Mom on the streets a couple of times over the next months. She would be out walking in the snow, a scarf pulled high around her face, and I figured she was looking for me.

Once she came up to where I was standing with a couple of guys. She reached out to put her hand on my arm, and I caught a glimpse of her eyes. I shoved her away.

"Don't come after me!"

"Sonny, you can't run from God. He is your answer and one of these days you will understand that," Mom said with her eyes red from tears.

Then I watched her shrink down inside her worn coat and half run, half walk down the sidewalk toward home. I couldn't understand why she loved me. All I'd ever done was hurt her.

My Name is Heroin

My name is heroin – call me smack for short.
I entered this country without a passport.
Ever since then I've made lots of scum rich.
Some have been murdered and found in a ditch.
I'm more valued than diamonds, more treasured than gold,
Use me just once and you too will be sold.
I'll make a schoolboy forget his books,
I'll make a beauty queen forget her looks.
I'll take a renowned speaker and make him a bore.
I'll take your mother and make her a whore.
I'll make a schoolteacher forget how to teach.
I'll make a preacher not want to preach.
I'll take all your rent money and you'll be evicted.
I'll murder your babies or they'll be born addicted.
I'll make you rob, and steal and kill.
When you're under my power, you have no will.
Remember, my friend, my name is "Big H,"
If you try me one time you may never be free.

I've destroyed actors, politicians and many a hero.
I've decreased bank accounts from millions to zero.
I make shooting and stabbing a common affair.
Once I take charge, you won't have a prayer.
Now that you know me, what will you do?
You'll have to decide, it's all up to you.
The day you agree to sit in my saddle
The decision is one that no one can straddle.
Listen to me, and please listen well,
When you ride with heroin you are headed for hell.

—Author Unknown

Chapter Three

A New Life

One day, skinny and pale, with holes in both my shoes, I was standing on the sidewalk by the candy store waiting for a drug dealer.

Suddenly I saw a guy coming around the corner looking real sharp. *A narc!* I thought, and then I recognized him. It was Chino! I hadn't seen him around for a long time. I figured he'd been in prison. Even from a distance I could tell he'd put on weight and looked real clean.

"Hey, Chino, hey, Man!" I yelled and waved, and he waved back, heading in my direction.

"Sonny! Man, am I glad to see you!" He smiled and pounded me on the shoulder.

"Why don't you stick around? I'm waiting for my connection to bring me an ounce. We can cut it, fix you up, and give you some extra for tomorrow," I said.

"Listen, Sonny, we been friends a long time. But if

you're gonna talk to me about anything, don't talk to me about drugs."

"Sure," I said. "You've been on the inside for a while."

"No, Sonny, I haven't been in prison — I'm clean! I haven't taken dope or smoked or had anything to drink for a year!"

"Listen, Chino, you and I are chips off the same rotten block. You might fool a square or someone who doesn't know you, but not me, not another junkie. Why, we've shot stuff together, we've robbed, we've stolen — you're not really telling me you don't use stuff anymore?"

"I'm not a doper anymore, Sonny. It's true. Let me tell you what happened to me, Man."

"Sure," I said. "I'm listening."

"I had gotten so sick and tired of hustling for dope and always running from the cops that I'd decided to commit suicide one evening. I went up on the roof of my apartment building and was going to jump off when I heard music.

"It was coming from a little storefront church on the other side of the street. It was as if something grabbed me and was pulling me back from the edge of the roof.

"I ran down the stairs and across the street and went into the church. I walked up the aisle without looking to either side, and up there at the altar I fell down and started to cry. It wasn't anything I'd decided to do; it was more like something happening to me that I didn't have any control over."

Chino was smiling. "I gave my heart to Jesus Christ that night, Sonny," he said. "And Jesus took away my dope addiction, my smoking habit, and my drinking. He filled me with His Holy Spirit, and I don't have to lie or steal no more or be afraid of getting arrested."

"Nothing can change a junkie," I said. "That's impossible, Man!"

Chino shook his head, stuck his hands deep in his trouser pockets, and shrugged his shoulders as if he wasn't about to argue with me.

"If you don't believe me," he said, "come with me to the Center and meet my new friends."

"Sure, I'll come with you," I said.

It was hard to believe that he had really changed. If he was a phony I wanted to be the one to expose him. When he said "the Center" I thought it was a term for a dance hall, smoking pot, and taking pills. As we walked down the street, Chino kept talking about his new life, how clean and pure he felt. I let him talk. It sounded great, but I knew the score.

Several times I saw his lips moving, like he was talking to himself or maybe praying about something.

Suddenly I remembered the ounce of heroin. I had forgotten about it. I'd need it soon, to avoid the death-pains of withdrawal.

"Chino, I got to go back and get my heroin!"

"We're almost there, Sonny, you're not gonna be sorry — we've got something better at the Center than you got back there. You won't need the ounce this time."

"This is it." Chino stopped in front of a three-story brick house. We stepped into a hallway first, and it was empty.

"This way, Sonny." Chino opened a door to the left and pushed me inside ahead of him. I found myself standing in an aisle. Several guys were sitting in chairs on both sides of the room, and up front was an altar with a cross. A guy was standing beside it, talking.

I was in church! What kind of a cheap trick was this?

"I thought you said we were going to a Teen Center," I whispered furiously to Chino.

"This is Teen Challenge Center," Chino said.

I wasn't going to listen; I'd heard enough from Mom and Dad about religion, and once I had run into that preacher on the street who tried to tell me Jesus could set me free from dope. I wasn't gonna get jinxed by any more Jesus talk. I sat down not wanting to create attention.

The guy up beside the altar was talking about the same thing—about how Jesus Christ could set you free from all kinds of hang-ups.

I got up from my seat and stumbled down the aisle toward the door.

"Where do you think you're going?" The voice that stopped me had great authority and a heavy accent.

Directly in front of me, with his hands on his hips and his feet planted squarely in the aisle, stood a dark-complexioned, curly-haired, Puerto Rican fellow. He was staring me in the eyes, and his head was thrust forward over a powerful set of shoulders. He looked like he was ready to fight.

"Hey you, wait a second!" he blurted in broken English, backing off and holding up his hand in a gesture of peace. "You know something, Man? You're nothing but a dirty drug addict, and you need help. God's help. Jesus Christ!"

Who does this creep think he is? I'm a drug addict, but not a dirty one. I felt like decking him right there, but I held back.

He pointed to an empty chair next to the aisle where we were standing. "Kneel down. I want to pray for you."

To my own surprise, I knelt by the chair without objection, thinking, *Who's afraid of prayer? A little prayer can't do me any harm. I'll let this crazy guy pray, and then I'll split from here.*

The fellow put his hands on my shoulders and prayed. "I was the leader of the Mau Mau Gang, and You changed me, Lord. Now I ask You to do it for this drug addict. Show him that You're real. Show him how dirty he is, how needy he is. Thank You Lord, in the name of Jesus Christ, Amen."

This guy couldn't be Nicky Cruz, who had terrorized Brooklyn and waged a one-man war with the police! Or could it? He was still standing with his hands on my shoulders.

"There's a room upstairs," he said. "I want you to come up there and stay till God has done His work in you.

"I can tell by looking at you that you are near the end of your rope. Jesus is the answer. I found Him and if I could, you can too."

I knew Nicky's reputation. *Maybe there's something to this stuff. What the heck, I need a bed for the night,* I thought.

"Okay, I'll stay for a little while — but I'm not gonna promise to change. I'll just stick around a couple of days maybe."

As soon as I saw the little room upstairs where Nicky took me, I was sorry I'd agreed to stay. Nicky was real excited.

"So, why don't you lie down and get some rest? I'll read some Bible to you." I could tell it wouldn't do any good for me to say no.

"I'm going to pray that God will heal you right now," he said. "You're not gonna get sick like before." He had no idea that I'd been using for six straight months. It was going to take me at least two weeks to kick my habit. My thoughts were in agony just thinking of the pain that was waiting for me up ahead.

I looked at him and shook my head in disgust at his ignorance of the facts.

"Go ahead; be my guest," I said. I closed my eyes and turned to the wall. I felt Nicky's hands on my head and shoulder. A warm, tingling sensation seemed to flow through them into me. I felt myself go rigid with fear. This was like nothing I'd ever experienced before...then without realizing it, I went to sleep.

I sat upright in bed. What was happening? Outside the window a pale glow of morning was touching the eastern sky. I looked around the room, and for a moment I couldn't remember where I was. I was sitting in a bed with nice, clean sheets, and I wasn't feeling any pain.

I leaped onto the floor and stretched my arms up over my head and it hit me: *Man, I'm supposed to be sick! Something's sure wrong!* Something weird was happening to me, and I was frightened.

"Nicky! Nicky!" I yelled. "Something's wrong, Man! I'm supposed to be sick, and I don't feel nothing except this weird feeling inside like something is bugging me. I'm really afraid!."

Nicky started laughing. "It's Jesus, Sonny. You're not a drug addict anymore. Jesus Christ has set you free."

I said, "Nobody ever kicked a habit without getting sick. Maybe I'm gonna get sick later."

"Sonny, I'm telling you the truth. You don't ever have to get sick again or take dope either. Jesus Christ is for real, Man, and He's doing the same thing today that this Bible says He did a long time ago. Listen to this.

"'But he was wounded for our transgressions, he was

bruised for our iniquities; the chastisement of our peace was upon him, and with his stripes we are healed'" (Isa. 53:5).

Nicky looked at me. "Don't you get it? Jesus took the rap for our rebellion and for our sins, and He even hung on that Cross for our sicknesses."

"What's the hitch? Why would Jesus want to die for a dirty drug addict?"

"Because He loves you, Sonny," Nicky said quietly.

"Me, Man? Jesus loves me? You gotta be kidding!"

"Why do you think He healed you? He did it just to give you the proof that He's for real. He wants you to turn your life over to Him."

The heavy feeling inside me was getting worse; it was like something was gonna burst any minute.

"Look, Sonny," Nicky said. "Jesus saved me when I was the meanest, toughest guy in Brooklyn, with nothing but hate in my heart. I've been to Bible school, and now I'm out on the streets telling other guys what Jesus can do for them. Man, Jesus can really use people like you and me."

Sweat broke out all over me. Then all at once I got control of myself and scrambled to my feet.

"Man, you guys are brainwashing me!" I was angry, embarrassed. "You think I'm going for this? You're trying to make me feel sorry for myself. I'm getting out of here!"

"I'm not trying to do anything, Sonny," he said. God

wants to set you free from your addiction."

I didn't want to hear any more. I ran down the stairs leaving Nicky behind. Then a voice spoke up from the back of my mind:

"So you're thinking of selling out to Jesus, Sonny. That means goodbye to all the good times. You're not gonna like it."

A couple of fellows came from the dining room, and I heard Chino's voice:

"Praise the Lord! He's touched Sonny."

Without warning, my eyes watered and a tear came down my face. I could feel my face getting hot with shame. I was really acting like a fool — right in front of Chino and those other guys. To escape, I ran for the nearest door and found myself in the chapel.

I wiped the tear off my face with the back of my hand and bit my lip till I wanted to cry out in pain.

Inside, I felt like I was being pulled one way and pushed the other. I wanted to let go, but something was holding me back, like an iron ring squeezing around my heart.

Man, I thought, if this thing is really God working on me, I don't want to fight it any longer.

"God," I said out loud, "it's true that I'm just a dirty drug addict like Nicky said. If You really sent Your Son to die on the Cross for every dirty thing I've done, I thank You, God, and I want You to come into my life and take over."

49

As soon as I said that, I overflowed with joy, because God was now flushing out all the junk: the hardness, the filth, and the loneliness. I threw myself down on the floor in front of the altar and cried and sobbed.

I don't know how long I stayed there. When I got up and looked at them — Chino, Nicky, and some other guys — I suddenly had a real warm feeling for them come up inside me. I thought, I'm different; I never cared for nobody before.

"Man," I said, "I think I just got saved! Am I saved, Man?"

"You're saved alright," they said laughing.

I started laughing then, too. Then I sobered and said, "If I'm saved, then I want Mom and Dad to be the first to know. They have been praying for this day for years!"

Sonny right after he was saved.

Before we left, the men formed a prayer circle around me, praying that my visit and talk with my parents would be a good one. "Please, God," I also prayed, "help them to believe me, please!" Chino and a staff worker, named Carl, went with me.

As we approached my parents' apartment, I said to the guys with me, "Keep out of sight until I motion for you to come in, but keep praying! They told me I could come and visit them anytime I wanted, but they didn't want any of my addict friends in the house."

I knocked on the door and Mom opened it. She looked real surprised, and stared at my puffed-up eyes. I started to go in, and she caught a glimpse of Chino and Carl as they stood in the hallway. Her hands went up, and I knew she was gonna yell and tell us all to get lost.

"Mom," I said quickly, "I gave my heart to Jesus this morning."

"What did you say?" Mom's eyes grew wide, and she stood there with her hands still up in the air.

"It's true, Mom, it's true!" I said. "I'm not the same guy anymore. Jesus Christ has come into my life."

Mom must have sensed that I was telling the truth, for her eyes filled up with tears, and she thrust her hands up higher and said, "Praise You, Jesus."

While her hands were raised, she started praying, "Dear God, for so many years now as I asked You to save Sonny. I knew You heard me, but it has seemed so long! I Praise You now, for Your faithfulness in saving my boy. Thank You, Jesus, thank You!"

Then she broke down and started crying real hard. She hid her face in her hands and her whole body shook with sobs.

As she was praying, I was suddenly overwhelmed with love for her. How she and Dad had suffered because of me! My lips started quivering and my body shook as I tried to say the words, "I love you, Mom." I thought everything inside me was going to explode. Her sweet, precious eyes were destroying me. As I sobbed, the words softly and slowly surfaced. "I love you, Mom," then like an erupting volcano, I screamed, "I LOVE YOU, MOM!" I grabbed her around the waist, picked her up, and swirled her around the room, still yelling, "I love you, I love you, I love you!"

"Sonny, put me down, put me down," Mom said, crying and laughing at the same time.

Chino and Carl, by this time, had come into the house and were rejoicing at seeing my mom and I embracing and praising God.

I finally put her down and stood there holding her, repeating over and over again, "Mom, I love you," as the tears were flowing down my face. I hadn't said those words since I was a little boy, and Mom cried even harder.

Finally Mom stopped crying and looked up at Carl and Chino with a bright gleam in her eye.

"Mom, they're Christians, too," I chuckled.

"Good. Thank God. Now let's have some coffee and talk," she said. "Your dad just went out to get some fresh doughnuts. We'll have to celebrate."

When Dad came home we were all in the kitchen laughing and talking, and every so often we'd stop and say, "Praise God," and "Thank You, Jesus." Dad stood in the doorway and looked like he had just fallen from outer space.

"What did I tell you, Papa? God touched Sonny; he's a Christian now," Mom shouted through her radiant smile.

Dad gave me a bear hug and blew his nose several times in a big white handkerchief while I told him what had happened at Teen Challenge.

"I'm going to stay at the Center for a while," I told them, "until I know what God wants me to do."

A few days later Carl went to see my mother. While he was there, my married sister, Judy, came home for a visit. Mom told her the news about me. My sister grew white as a sheet and said, "If Sonny has given his heart to Jesus, it can only mean one thing: It must be the end of the world, Jesus must be coming again real soon." My sister started crying and trembling with fear.

Carl put his hand on her shoulder and asked, "Would you like to ask Jesus into you life right now?" Judy nodded, and right there at the kitchen table, she also gave her life to Jesus Christ.

Chapter Four

Living for God

I was the first heroin addict to be converted at the Center. I learned that the workers and converts at Teen Challenge had been praying for some time about a breakthrough in the work with addicts.

"Wilkerson is gonna shout praises to heaven when he hears about you!" Nicky said. We were having coffee in the dining room the day after my conversion.

"Who's Wilkerson?" I asked.

"The preacher, David Wilkerson, the guy who started this place a couple of years ago."

"Is he a tall, skinny kind of guy who used to run around on the street telling everybody that Jesus could set them free?" I asked.

"Yeah, that's him," said Nicky. "Did you run into him before?"

I almost spilled my coffee.

"Man, did I!" I said. "If it's the guy I think it is, he got to me one night when I was too stoned to care.

"That tall, serious-looking fellow had been coming to our neighborhood for some time, carrying his Bible and talking to us about Jesus. Of course we didn't believe he was really a preacher. We'd met narcos in clever disguises before, and nobody on the street took the guy seriously. The last time I saw him, about two years ago, I jumped out of his car and ran down the street."

Nicky said, "Sonny, Wilkerson slept here last night. Come with me, I want him to see you."

As we walked into his office, our eyes met. He immediately recognized me. I could see a look of surprise on his face. He got up and walked toward me saying, "Sonny, it's really you! I had heard that the Lord had miraculously delivered a young man from Brooklyn named Sonny, and I wondered if you were that same person."

Wilkerson put his arm on my shoulder and said, "I've been praying for you, Sonny. It's amazing to see how God answers prayer."

At that moment I was overwhelmed by the love and compassion of David. I remembered how he tried so hard to reach me years before and how I refused to listen.

The three of us sensed the Lord's presence in a special way. David said, "Come on boys, let's thank the Lord for His miracle."

We gathered in a circle and David gave a prayer of

thanksgiving to God. As tears streamed down my face, I thanked God for allowing me to be a part of such a loving and compassionate family.

In the midst of my exciting new life, I was still aware of the burglary charge pending against me.

I could tell the truth or a lie. Since this was my tenth arrest, I couldn't expect leniency from the judge if he should find me guilty.

Deep down I knew what the answer had to be. Telling a lie would amount to a denial of Jesus Christ. I told my lawyer that I would answer truthfully any question asked me in court. He shook his head in disgust.

"You're being a fool, Sonny," he said. "If you plead guilty on this one, you might as well prepare yourself for a nice, long term in prison."

"Okay," I acknowledged, "but that's not my problem. I've got to tell the truth. The rest is up to God."

David Wilkerson had called Paul DiLena, a police captain who was a friend of Teen Challenge. He had come with me to court. When the judge asked me to come forward, Captain DiLena came with me. The judge looked at him and asked, "Are you a lawyer?"

DiLena answered, "No, Your Honor, I'm a police captain, and I'm here on my own time with Sonny because I've known him for several months.

"Sonny came to Teen Challenge Center and met Jesus Christ as his personal Saviour. Now Sonny isn't on drugs anymore; instead he's out on the streets with other Teen Challenge workers talking to young people about how they can be set free through a personal relationship with Jesus."

I looked at the judge, who was listening very carefully. The courtroom was so quiet you could hear the traffic on the street below.

The judge said seriously, "I presume you know Sonny's previous record in this court?"

"Yes, Your Honor, I do."

The judge looked thoughtful, and I was praying under my breath:

"God, You know what's best for me. Your will be done, and just give me the strength to stay in Your will, Lord."

Finally the judge told us to come back for the afternoon session, when the district attorney would be there, and also the arresting officer.

That afternoon there were three judges present when Captain DiLena and I were called forward. As we went up front, I saw my father and mother. Whatever the outcome, for the first time in my life I knew that my dad was proud that I was his son. His eyes met mine for a short moment, and there was a hint of a smile as he nodded at me across the courtroom.

Quickly I turned my head. I didn't want him to see the tears of joy suddenly flooding my eyes.

The three judges put their heads together, talking about what to do with me. They called on the district attorney, who said that he would certainly go along with their decision. The arresting officer agreed. Finally, the presiding judge looked at me, then at Captain DiLena.

"We find it difficult to believe that Sonny has really been rehabilitated to the extent you claim. He has a long record in this court, and is known as a confirmed drug addict. However, we respect your record with the police department and feel that you would not take it upon yourself to defend Sonny unless you were convinced that a real change had taken place. We will let him go."

The judge turned and looked directly at me. "If you're playing a game, Sonny," he warned, "you'll soon be back in this court. And you can be sure we'll give you a double sentence! Case dismissed!"

I was free! For the first time in my life I was free to look forward to a future with no threat of a prison term hanging over my head.

I continued hitting the streets with Nicky. We went out trying to reach the gang members on the streets at random. We weren't having much success with gang members, so I told him, "Man, I know a whole lot of people that really need Jesus. I know these guys. I'll go testify, and then you preach to them." So we teamed up together, and went back to my old neighborhood. Nicky soon realized everybody knew me. Well, almost everybody.

We started having street meetings, using a P.A.

system. I got up and said, "You guys remember me? I used to walk along these streets, and burn you people, steal from you, and break into your apartments. You know how crazy I was before. I was a junkie like many of you who are listening. Well, I want to tell you, Jesus changed my life. This ex-gang leader prayed for me, and I gave my life to Jesus."

Sonny praying with two young men.

When I ran out of words, and I didn't know what else to say, Nicky got up and he started telling them about Jesus. "If you want Jesus to come into your heart right now, He'll set you free. He'll change your life." To our amazement, suddenly most of these guys started responding. They came down from the roof-tops, out of the alleys, from everywhere. They knelt with us on the sidewalk and prayed the sinner's prayer. It was awe-some. We had a Teen Challenge van parked nearby. Nicky said, "Those of you who want to be set free from your drug habits and know more about Jesus, we want you to come with us. Get in the van."

Six of them got in the van and we took them back to the Center and into the chapel. We prayed deliverance over them.

Revival broke out among the drug addicts. I developed a burden for them, and also for the gang members. God began to move in a very powerful way. I stayed at Teen Challenge for seven months.

Since I didn't know what my future was going to be, I started getting frustrated. The whole thing was suddenly boring to me, and I felt less and less inclined to spend time in Bible reading and prayer.

Nicky had been watching me with growing concern, and I'd avoided talking to him. But one day he cornered me and asked, "What's wrong, Sonny?" He looked at me, and I tried to keep from looking back at him.

"Nothing, maybe I'm just through with the program and getting ready to leave."

"Where would you go?" Nicky asked.

"Don't know," I shrugged. "Back home to get a job, maybe."

A couple of days later Wilkerson called me into his office. When I got there, Nicky was leaning up against the wall, and both of them looked serious.

"How would you like to go to Bible school, Sonny?" Wilkerson asked.

"Bible school?" I questioned. "I don't know. I dropped out of school in the eighth grade. What would I do in Bible school?"

"Do you feel that God has called you to work for Him?" Nicky prodded.

I felt the heat go to my head.

"Yeah," I mumbled. "So what?"

"Bible school is a wonderful preparation," Wilkerson said with enthusiasm. "Three years with a wonderful bunch of young people, and a chance to really dig in and learn about the Bible. It's the best way to learn good study habits and self-discipline."

Nicky was looking at me and smiling.

"I know what you're thinking, Sonny," he said. "I don't like that discipline bit either, but without it we're no good to ourselves or to the Lord."

"We think you'll really like going to La Puente Bible School," Wilkerson added, as if the whole thing was settled already.

"La Puente!" I said. "I've never been to California!"

Nicky leaned across Wilkerson's desk. "Sonny, why don't you pray about it?"

I went to the chapel, but all I could muster was a half-hearted prayer, "God, if You want me at La Puente, please let me be admitted and You provide the way."

It was a chore to think about the future. Maybe if I

went to Bible school, I wouldn't have to make any big decisions for a while.

I told Nicky and Wilkerson to go ahead and apply for my admission to school. Nicky and his wife Gloria were all excited about my decision.

"You'll love it," Gloria said. She had asked Nicky to bring me home for dinner, and I sat in their cozy little apartment and listened as they talked for hours about the school. Sure, they *can talk*, I thought. *They have it made*. They had met at Bible school, and their future was all mapped out. Gloria was pregnant now with their first baby, and everything looked settled and happy.

"Who knows, Sonny?" Gloria giggled and served me a second piece of cake. "Maybe you'll meet a girl at Bible school!"

I wouldn't have known what to do if I had met a girl. I'd never been around a Christian girl. At the Center we weren't allowed to talk privately to the girls, and the only kind of boy-girl relationship I'd ever known was out on the streets.

Before long, word came back that I was accepted at the school, the money was provided through the Center, and I was all set to go. That is, the arrangements were settled; I was not. I was feeling increasingly edgy and uncomfortable.

I thought, *Dave and Nicky are just trying to get me away from here. They're afraid I'm gonna go back on the*

*street and ruin the reputation of the Center. They don't
really care about me.*

I sat in chapel one morning feeling miserably sorry
for myself, and suddenly David Wilkerson got up to
preach.

"I'm afraid," he said, "that some of you guys are
slacking off on your prayer life and Bible reading.
Watch out! That's when the enemy gets to you, and you
start getting restless and bored and wanting to go back
out on the street."

I felt he was looking straight at me and I thought,
*Man, this is too much. He ought to be decent enough not
to talk about me like that in front of everybody.*

Still seething over the injustice I'd suffered, I decided to leave. I took the subway and got home just as
Mom was ready to go shopping.

"What are you doing home, Sonny?" She looked at my
suitcase and then searchingly at my face. "Something
wrong?"

"Of course not, Mom." I tried to laugh. "Everything is
great at the Center. I just thought I'd spend a couple of
days at home."

Mom didn't look quite convinced, but she didn't say
anything more. I put my suitcase down in the bedroom
and headed for the street.

The street was the same as it had always been — the
familiarity was tugging at me. Was this where I be-
longed?

There was a rustling noise in the alley's dark shadow. Two figures were huddled by the wall; one of them looked up and called out, "Hey Sonny! How you doin'?"

Dukie and Ray were squatting, and I saw the glimmer of metal in Dukie's hand before the needle jabbed into his arm.

"Wow, Man!" Dukie leaned back against the brick wall and smiled. "That stuff sure makes you feel good. How about it, Sonny? Wanna try it? Or are you still trippin' with Jesus?"

What was I doing? Dreaming of the freedom in a needle? Freedom at the bottom of a hellhole, like a monkey on a choke collar with the devil holding the leash? *Oh God, help me!*

A wave of nausea caught me by surprise, and I leaned over, grasping my stomach with both hands. The vomit sailed in a stream, splashing over my shoes and over Dukie's and Ray's outstretched legs. They didn't seem to notice, and I turned, running back into the street as if the devil himself were after me.

I walked quickly down the sidewalk. There were guys and girls I knew, and they called after me:

"Hi, Sonny. How are you doing, Sonny?" I had often stopped to talk to them before, when I'd been out witnessing with Nicky or some of the other fellows from Teen Challenge.

Turning a corner, I nearly ran into a guy walking in the other direction.

"Sonny!" The guy stopped and grabbed my shoulder.

"Chino!" I was so relieved I grabbed hold of him, and we just stood there. "Man, am I glad to see you!" I said.

Chino looked worried. "What's happening, Sonny?" he said. "What are you doing out here?"

I suddenly remembered the humiliation of morning chapel, and the anger made a tight knot in my stomach.

"I'm bugged!" I said. "Those people at Teen Challenge have it in for me, Man. This morning in chapel Wilkerson let me have it from the pulpit — right in front of everybody!"

"Look, Sonny," he said seriously, "you shouldn't be out here and you know it."

"That's the trouble with us addicts," Chino was saying. "We're used to running out every time something goes against us, like we used to run to the needle," he continued.

"Every time I get discouraged, I know I'm gonna get tempted to fall back. But every time I stick it out, I get a little stronger."

It was after midnight when we stopped at a cafeteria for something to eat. I was munching my ham sandwich when somebody stopped next to our table.

He stood, feet apart and planted squarely on the floor, hands on his hips, and head thrust forward as if he was ready to fight. I had seen him that way before — in the chapel at Teen Challenge.

"Nicky! What are you doing here?"

"Sonny, what are you doing here? I've been looking for you all day, and so has Wilkerson."

I looked down. "I'm not coming back. Those people back there are really bugging me." I told him then what Wilkerson had said during morning chapel.

"Man," he said, "Dave wasn't talking to you personally. Why don't you go tell him how you feel about it?" he said.

"You can tell him."

"Come on, Sonny. Are you gonna be man enough to tell Wilkerson what you think of him?"

Defiantly, I rose to my feet. "Sure, I'll tell him," I said. "Let's go."

Back at the Teen Center, we had barely walked through the door of his office when I blurted out, "I didn't like the way you put me down in front of everybody in chapel!"

David looked surprised. "I what? Don't you see, Sonny? I wasn't talking to you, the Holy Spirit was showing you your own weaknesses. If you'd stayed around for the rest of the chapel service, you would have seen that almost all the fellows came up to the altar for prayer. They, too, felt that I was speaking to them."

I took his hand in both of mine and felt a wave of warmth and relief flow over me. "Jesus!" I cried out loud. "Jesus, I'm sorry. I don't want to chicken out on You."

Dave then said, "Sonny, I feel you should go to California tomorrow. I'm going to send Nicky with you, to make sure you get there."

Chapter Five

TWO BECOME ONE

Julie:

A few months after I was converted, I attended a church service with my mom and dad. The preacher shared about the need for laborers. "Look on the fields. The fields are ripe, ready for harvest," he said.

He fervently preached on the tremendous need for laborers, and pleaded for those among the congregation to give their lives to be missionaries. I sat there, wanting to go forward, thinking *I am only seventeen, what do I have to offer to God?* After his continued plea, I felt the nudge of the Spirit and was the last one to go to the altar. The speaker came to me and said, "Young girl, God is going to use you some day. He has His hand on your life."

At that moment, I truly felt the call of God. The burning desire to learn more of the Word of God was kindled in my heart, so I soon enrolled in Bible school.

I was saved in a denomination that was very strict and legalistic. Women didn't cut their hair and wore it piled on top of their heads or in a bun. The Bible school was really strict, and we were expected to pray about five hours each day. Those principles, though hard, were very good for me because I learned how to pray. I only attended there one year.

The second year I went to the Latin American Bible Institute in La Puente, California. When I got there I didn't think anybody was saved because they didn't pray like I was used to praying. Also, the girls cut their hair and wore a little makeup. I told them, "This is not what God wants, this is worldly." They thought I was a fanatic because I would stay in the chapel for hours, praying. Most of them didn't know that kind of prayer life. To put it bluntly, I was somewhat self-righteous.

During vacations, I took every opportunity I had to be in Mexico, trying to do something for the Lord.

I had finished my second year of Bible school, when I got a magazine in the mail from Teen Challenge in New York. It had Sonny Arguinzoni's testimony in it.

When I read it I received a lot of faith for my brother Gary. He had gone back to using drugs, even though he had been exposed to the gospel. I started praying for Gary and kept that testimony with Sonny's picture on it pinned on my wall. I prayed for him every day, because the article asked that we pray for him, as he needed our prayers.

He lived in New York, three thousand miles away. I had never even left Los Angeles, other than going to Mexico for missionary work, so I never thought I'd get to meet him.

When I started my third year at Bible school, Gary, my brother, had just been saved about three weeks before school started. Miraculously, they let him attend the Bible school. I was so excited and praised God for that wonderful miracle in his life. Gary had now given his life completely to the Lord.

At the first assembly of the school year, all first year students would go up front, give their name and a short testimony. When I saw Gary go up there and give his name, I was telling everybody, "That's my brother! God is truly a God of miracles. You are seeing a miracle." After Gary, another young man walked up front, and did he look rough! Something similar to my brother Gary — that rough, drug addict look. He had a leather jacket on, and walked up front, real confident, with that strutting walk. "My name is Sonny Arguinzoni, and I'm from New York City," he said.

That's the young man I've been praying for every day! I can't believe it. I just can't believe that it's really him! I eagerly thought.

After the service was over I went up to him and excitedly asked, "Sonny, are you the one I read about in the Teen Challenge magazine? I've been praying for you every day."

He looked at me with disinterest and said, "Yeah, why?" I had my hair up in a little bun, like a good little Pentecostal — "holiness personified."

I continued, "Because I've been praying for you everyday and...." I hadn't even finished my sentence when his eyes turned away from me and he was greeting someone else. I felt like such a fool. Here I was so excited and he didn't even care what I had to say. After that incident, I tried to avoid him as much as possible.

Sonny:

When I got to La Puente Bible School I found myself with a totally different crowd...they all spoke, read, and wrote in Spanish.

In class I had to read in Spanish, I had to write in Spanish, and I had to speak in Spanish. That was very difficult because I didn't know how to read, write, or speak Spanish. The Bible was in Spanish. The books were in Spanish. The tests were in Spanish. Everything was in Spanish. All teaching was in Spanish. I couldn't handle it so I called Wilkerson and said, "Dave, you made a mistake, Man. Why did you send me to this place? It's all in Spanish. I understand very little of it, and I'm flunking my exams. Dave, you made a mistake, send me a plane ticket, I'm coming back home."

Wilkerson answered, "No, Sonny, I'm not sending you anything. It's God's will for you to be there, and you just stick it out and don't worry about it, God will see you through. There's nothing more to talk about. That's it. God will see you through," and Dave hung up the phone.

That was it! I went to the chapel, and I began to pray:

"Jesus, if You really want me here, then Lord, teach me how to read, write, and speak Spanish."

My education had ended after the eighth grade. That's as far as I went in school. Also, I had not been in school for a number of years, so I was a little rusty, to say the least. Gradually, God began to open up my mind, and as I was reading the Bible in Spanish, I began to understand it. It was miraculous. I started reading it more and more, and then I began getting better grades.

There was a student in my class that I immediately recognized as an ex-drug addict. His name was Gary. We became friends, and he took me out to his old neighborhood and that's when I started noticing the need in Los Angeles. I still didn't have a heavy burden for L.A. because I always felt that I was to go back to New York City, and work there.

When I met Julie Rivera, Gary's sister, I was impressed with her. Her innocent look intrigued me. She was sure different from the other girls I had met.

After much prayer I finally got up enough nerve to talk to the president of the Bible school. "Sir, I have a real burden to form an evangelistic team and hit the troubled areas of Los Angeles with the gospel. If I could get a pastor to sponsor us, would you be open to it?" I asked.

He thought for a moment then said, "Sonny, if you find a pastor to sponsor the team, I will give my permission."

The school team — Sonny, third from right; Julie, first from right.

I not only got a pastor to sponsor the team, but he had a vehicle that we were able to use. We came and approached the president of the school and he gave his consent. We were able to have guys and girls from the school go out and evangelize the streets. We began to have street meetings among the addicts and gang members. Out of all that evangelism, Teen Challenge of Los Angeles was born. We also teamed up with another guy from Southern California College who had a team in the streets and he became the first director of the Teen Challenge Center there.

Julie:

Long before I met Sonny, I had direction in my life. I was positive that I was going to be a missionary. Then things changed. When I would pray, Sonny's face would flash before my mind. I'd be studying, and Sonny's face would come to my mind.

What is happening to me? I thought. *He never looked at me or hardly noticed that I was alive. The devil must have brought him into my life. The enemy is trying to divert my thoughts, he is trying to get me out of God's will and that's wrong!*

I never thought that Sonny was for me. Not only because of my direction in life, but because he had been a junkie, and I had vowed that I would never marry a junkie. No matter if he was saved, I would never marry somebody from that lifestyle. I knew what they were like, and if they go back to drugs, forget it! My sister had married a junkie, and she suffered a life of torment. But I couldn't get him off my mind. I prayed, "Oh, my God! Help me!" I was in absolute turmoil and anguish. I could hardly read the Bible or pray. Most of all I never wanted to be out of God's will.

In desperation I went to the president of the school and told him, "Sir, I really need to get away for a while. I have something to pray about. I have been going through this problem for about two-and-a-half months, and I need to hear from God." He told me I could take a week off.

I went home and said to my mother, "I'm going to lock myself up in my room, pray and fast, and ask God for an answer." I didn't tell her what I would be praying about, because I was too embarrassed. Sonny had never looked at me or anything. I was trying to get him out of my life, not into my life, thinking that my thoughts were of the devil. I knew I had to get free from those thoughts, so I stayed in my room fasting and praying.

The first day I prayed, "Oh, God, take this guy out of my thoughts. Lord, I have my direction, I want to serve You. I want to be a missionary, Lord, please."

The second day I prayed the same. I continued night and day, night and day.

The third day, about four o'clock in the morning as I was praying again, I said, "Lord, take these thoughts of him out of my mind."

Then the Lord spoke clearly to me, and said, "No, Julie. Sonny is going to be your husband."

"He's going to be my WHAT?" I exclaimed.

"He is going to be your husband. And it's going to be

very hard for you. Are you willing?"

"Lord, my husband? You know I wasn't praying about marriage, or dating, or anything. Just my thoughts of him. My husband!"

He asked again, "Are you willing? It is going to be very difficult."

"Lord, if that's Your will for my life, I'm willing. Of course, I'm willing." I looked at my watch and thought, *I barely have enough time to go to chapel. I want to go and take another good look at Sonny.*

I got dressed, kissed my mom goodbye, and hurried as fast as I could to get to the chapel early, and I sat in a place where I could see Sonny real good. I looked at his face, his ears, his hands, his big feet, and said to myself, *He doesn't even know it, but he's gonna be my husband.*

A lot of girls at school liked him because he was a novelty. He was different from all the other guys at school because of his background. Sonny was also preaching everywhere. They wanted him to go here and there, and he was getting packages in the mail from all over the country. It was like he was the most famous one in school. A lot of the girls thought he was pretty neat, and he had a following, but I was secure in my heart because God had told me that I didn't have to do anything. I knew the Lord was going to put it together.

By now, everyone at school knew that David Wilkerson of *The Cross and the Switchblade* movie and Nicky Cruz were the two men who had brought Sonny to Jesus. Nicky Cruz was David Wilkerson's first gang member convert and Sonny was the first drug addict saved in his great Teen Challenge ministry.

Sonny was an active person and couldn't stand being idle. I could see him getting restless the second semester of school, so I was relieved when I heard about the evangelistic team that he was starting, and was anxious to be a part of it.

He asked me to be his secretary and I got a little closer to him. Eventually he asked me to go out on a date. We would only see each other once a month, but I had never met anyone like this man. None. I thought, *if I'm gonna date this fellow, I want to go to prayer for at least an hour before I go out with him, because I don't trust him. Even if he is converted and loves Jesus, he comes from a different lifestyle.*

We prayed every time we went out, because we didn't want to offend the Lord. We would be walking down the street and sometimes the Spirit of God would come on us, and we'd feel the presence of God so strong. One time we were sitting in front of my house talking about the Lord, and God's Spirit came on us, and we began weeping, crying, and praying. My brother came by and asked, "What's wrong? What happened?"

"It's just the Spirit of God all over us!" we responded.

Gary joined us praising the Lord. There were quite a few times that God revealed himself in our courtship. It was really, really special.

When I graduated from school, Sonny went back to New York. I went to work on the staff at the Teen Challenge Center for the summer. Sonny was in New York helping Nicky Cruz. Every so often we would write, or he would call. We weren't really committed to each other, just dating.

Sonny:

When I flew back to California by myself, there was one thing I had to get settled right away. Julie and I had written back and forth during the summer, and I felt it was time to propose and set a date for the wedding. I knew she was the one God had picked for me and I needed her. All summer long I'd been homesick for her. In her letters she'd talked mostly about what was happening at the new Teen Challenge Center, but she also mentioned a couple of times her dream of going to Mexico as a missionary. I'd felt a twinge of fear. What if she took off for Mexico when summer was over? She was certainly free to make her own decisions now that she had graduated from school.

Seeing her again was like a refreshing, cool breeze on a hot, summer day. She was prettier than I remembered, and I just wanted to hold her hand and look at her forever. We were standing outside her house and I just couldn't let go of her hand.

"Julie," I said, "I've got to ask you something," I said.

Her eyes were wide and serious with a glow in them. "What is it, Sonny?" she whispered.

"Will you marry me?" My heart was pounding way up in my throat.

"Oh, Sonny." Her voice was soft. "Oh, yes!"

"When?" I wanted it settled right away and Julie giggled.

"You've got to ask my father first, Sonny!"

"Your father? Can't you tell him?"

Julie shook her head. "Don't you know you're supposed to ask the father for his daughter's hand in marriage?" She was mock-serious and pulled me toward the porch steps.

"Why don't you do it right away?"

I felt like a sheep being led to the slaughter. How do you propose to a girl's father?

Mr. Rivera was in the living room reading the newspaper. He looked up when we came through the doorway.

"Hi, Sonny! Good to have you back!" After the greeting, he went back to reading his newspaper, and I stood in the middle of the floor, shifting my weight from one foot to the other, not knowing what to say next.

By some secret and instant communication, Mrs. Rivera seemed to understand that Julie wanted her out of there and the two of them disappeared toward the kitchen, giggling, and looking back at me.

I cleared my throat and Julie's dad looked up again. "I'd like to talk to you," I said.

He lowered the newspaper.

"Sure, Sonny, go right ahead." He smiled reassuringly, and I swallowed hard.

I thought, Man, what *do I tell him? I haven't got anything to offer his daughter — no job, no money, and I've got two more years to go in school.* There was an old army picture of Gary on the wall and I stared at it, tongue-tied.

Abel Rivera was looking at me. "Sit down, Sonny," he nodded toward the couch. "You got a problem or something?" He looked concerned.

"Yes, I mean, no." I felt flustered. "I just want to ask for Julie's hand in marriage." There, it was done. After I had blurted it out, he leaned back on the couch and smiled.

I thought, *Now he's gonna ask me how I plan to support her.*

"Have you prayed about it?" her father asked. I nodded. "Do you both feel this is God's will?" I nodded again, and he looked at me thoughtfully. "It isn't easy to be in the ministry," he said slowly. "Choosing the right wife is important. She's got to be right for you and you for her because you're going to serve God as a team."

I nodded. "God did the choosing," I said, and her father smiled like it was all settled. "When is the wedding gonna be, Sonny?"

I swallowed hard. "Next year?" I said, my voice cracking like an adolescent'

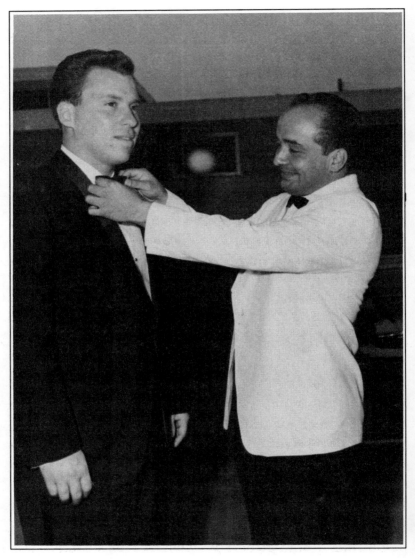

Sonny and Gary Rivera, Julie's brother.

"How about waiting till after you graduate?"

"We'd like to pray about it," I said. "Let the Lord set the time."

Mr. Rivera nodded and stretched out his hand. "Welcome to the family, Sonny. It's good to have you. I know you'll take good care of Julie." We shook hands, and I felt like I was about to burst inside. Man, I was gonna marry the prettiest, most wonderful girl in the whole world!

Julie and her mother were suddenly in the doorway.

"Congratulations!" Mrs. Rivera was beaming. "Come here and let me hug you."

That night, back in my room at school, I knelt by my bed. "Father," I prayed, "I praise You and thank You for Julie. Don't ever let me hurt her. Be the head of our family, Lord, and teach me to be the right kind of husband and provider."

Julie:

We had to wait for a whole year to be married, and that was a very difficult time for us. Because of the rules of school, we saw each other about once a month. Sonny was always on discipline at school, because he was constantly breaking the rules.

In those days, they were tough, really tough for a fast-lane man from New York City! Sonny had the zeal and ambition of five other men put together. He sometimes would go across the street for a Coke. That was a no-no, and then he would be put on discipline. He really wanted to change and he did, but it came bit by bit.

During that time, my parents were remarried.

Sonny and I didn't have any money, or hardly any possessions. My parents were just getting re-established themselves. They had my brother in school, and they still had two younger ones at home. So it was kind of difficult for them, too. However, Sonny and I went ahead and married on June 6, 1964.

Ruth and Betty, who were long-time friends of our family, and some of their friends said, "Let's put on a reception for these two."

They got different friends to make the cake, bring food, and do everything for us. It was a reception like none other.

Sonny and Julie on their wedding day.

We had a really beautiful wedding, with ten couples serving as our attendants. As we drove away for our honeymoon, a good feeling came over me and I thought, *I will never have to say goodbye to Sonny anymore! I'm going to be able to be with him always.*

Little did I know that I was just beginning to know him. To me, he was a perfect person. I didn't know his flaws. Before we were married, when we were together, he would be praying, or evangelizing; I saw only the good things. When we got married I started seeing the rough part of the diamond. I began to understand what the Lord meant when He told me it was going to be difficult. I didn't really know how difficult it was going to be, being Mrs. Sonny Arguinzoni.

Chapter Six

We Hear From God

We were married and with my going to school and all, we had a rough time of it. We were determined that I had to finish my last year of school and get my diploma.

I spent most of my weekends preaching, trying to bring in some money for our support. Julie was also working at the time, but then she got pregnant, and couldn't work anymore.

We were living in a small apartment off campus and at times we didn't have any money, and would go without. After much sacrifice and hardship, I finally graduated. By this time we had our first daughter, Debbie. Upon graduating I launched out into full-time ministry. I was a field evangelist for Teen Challenge. I would raise money and support for Teen Challenge around the country. After that, I worked with Nicky Cruz for a while.

When I was traveling with Nicky, we would go into

a city and big crowds and ministers would receive us at the airport. We were traveling first class. That was when *The Cross and the Switchblade* book had just come out, and we were doing very well. While I was traveling with him we would be gone for a week at a time, and then I would go home and stay for only a few days, then be gone again.

While I was traveling, deep inside there was something missing in my life. I felt that even though I was doing the work of the Lord, somehow I was out of the will of God.

God was using Nicky in a very powerful way. After the meetings I would leave the fellowship and take off to my hotel room, fall on my knees, and begin to weep. There was a heaviness inside of me, and I didn't know why. Then Nicky began to ask, "Man, what's bugging you. Tell me what's wrong with you?"

"I don't know, but I'm not happy. Something's happening inside, and I don't know what it is, but I'm just not happy," I responded.

Nicky said, "Well, man, you better get it together and find out what's wrong."

"Nicky," I said, "I'm gonna go back home, and I'm gonna be alone with God."

I told Julie, "I feel that I gotta find out what the Lord has for me. Even though I'm doing the work of God, somehow I'm still not happy. Something is missing inside, and I know I can't go on like this. It seems like

I'm out of the will of God. Honey, I'm gonna get alone with God to pray."

Julie had a relative who had a home in San Diego, I talked to him, and was able to use a room in his house. I wanted to get far away so that I could spend my time in prayer, uninterrupted.

I started praying and seeking the Lord asking, "Lord, why is it that I am so confused, why do I feel the way I do? Why is it that I'm going through this turmoil?" On the morning of the third day, the Lord spoke to my heart. He said, "The reason that you feel the way you do is because you're out of My will. You are doing My work, but you are still out of My divine will."

"Well, Lord," I asked, "what would You have me to do?"

The Lord answered, "I want you to open up a church. I want to fill it with drug addicts and their families."

One of the ministries that I never wanted to be involved in was pastoring! That was the furthest thing from my mind, because I knew I couldn't stay put in one place. I wanted to travel. I was discipled by Nicky, and another evangelist, David Wilkerson, who also had an influence in my life. I had never sat under a pastor, I had never, in all my Christian experience, been a member of any church. I didn't even know the first thing of how to run a church. But all of a sudden the Lord was speaking to me, and putting in my heart that He wanted me to open up a church, and He promised that He would fill it up with drug addicts and their families.

When I came back home Julie was waiting for me and asked, "Any word from the Lord?"

"Yep, He spoke to me," I said.

"Well, what did He say?" she asked in excitement.

"Julie," I told her, "He told me something very strange, and I am not too happy about what He wants me to do. He wants me to open up a church for drug addicts."

She responded, "A what? I've never heard of a church for drug addicts. You mean you are going to be a pastor?"

I said, "Yes, that's what God has told me to do."

She was happy about the pastor part, and said, "Now I can have you home most of the time, you don't have to be traveling. That's great. Well, where do we begin?"

"It can't be Los Angeles," I said. "I don't fully understand the street language or the culture. It has to be New York. I didn't ask God, and He didn't tell me, but it has to be New York, in my old stomping grounds, where I know everything about drugs, and what's happening there in the streets."

I told Julie, "Start packing, we're moving to New York!" In a few days I went to New York alone to scout the land. I went over to Teen Challenge and shared my vision with David Wilkerson about opening a church for drug addicts and their families.

When I spoke to Dave, he did not see the vision and told me, "Sonny, I'm afraid that we're a para-church organization, and I'm not about to get into opening up churches. Why don't you just work here in Teen Challenge, and then we'll see what happens down the road."

I said, "No David, I know what I'm supposed to do, so I've gotta do it."

I got a bunch of drug addicts from the streets of my old neighborhood and told them about the vision of opening up a church for them. "This is going to be a church for you," I said.

I rented a store front. I was ready to start getting into it. I told all the drug addicts, "This is going to be your church. We're gonna fix it up." So they went out, very excited, and began bringing in paint. Many of them probably stole the paint from somewhere, and some brought other materials. They were gonna have a church. These guys weren't even saved and I had them painting the church, and getting everything ready.

Suddenly, I began to have the same feeling that I had when I was out in the field with Nicky, as if I were out of the will of God.

I started praying, seeking God again. "Lord, why am I feeling like this again? You told me to come to New York to open up a church."

Then the Lord spoke to me, "I didn't tell you to come to New York. YOU told yourself to come to New York."

Then I realized what a foolish mistake I had made.

I called Julie and said, "Julie, you better unpack, somehow I have made a mistake."

"What do you mean?" she asked.

"I'll explain when I get home," I answered.

Then I told the guys who were out getting paint, "You better give all that stuff back. I made a mistake."

"What? What do you mean?" they asked.

I said, "Man, I made a mistake. I'm in the wrong place. I'm sorry. I'll see you guys." I felt like a blundering idiot as I left them and got on the first plane back to Los Angeles.

As I took my seat on the plane, a spirit of confusion seemed to come all over me. I wasn't sure if I was really hearing from God. Maybe I should have stayed in New York...I didn't know. During the entire flight, I fought this confusion and prayed.

When the plane landed in LA, and my feet touched the ground, the confusion was instantly gone. The Spirit of God came upon me and His still, small voice spoke, "Sonny, you said you couldn't reach the neighborhoods here, because you didn't know how to communicate with them. You didn't know their language or the culture. Sonny, this is the place where I have called you. You will not do it alone. I will equip you, and I am the One Who will do these wonderful things through you."

When I saw Julie I told her, "This is the place."

I had an awesome feeling of peace.

Chapter Seven

Gless Street

Julie and I moved into a low income government housing project. The rent was low, but the place was small. We began taking in addicts who needed a place to kick their habits, and began holding services in our living room.

Our apartment had two small bedrooms, and most of the time, one was occupied by one or more addicts. By this time God had blessed us with another little girl we named Doreen.

Julie:

One of the things that I appreciated about Sonny, even though he was rough in so many ways, was that I could see that he maintained a real good prayer life. I would hear him crying daily before the Lord, and he knew how to repent before God. He knew how to get hold of God and had developed an intimate relationship with Him. So, in spite of all the work that I discovered needed to be done in him, I knew that God really had His hand on his life, and was going to use him greatly. He had compassion for people, and tried so hard to help them, no matter what their problems were. Our relationship, in the beginning years, however, was strained, because we didn't have very good communication. Sonny just thought that I should be quiet and not take part in his decisions. He wanted to be left alone, so he could "do his thing" for the Lord. He didn't give me much say about anything, and that made me feel terrible.

He wouldn't allow me to get too involved in the ministry and would say, "You just take care of the house and the babies and I'll take care of the ministry."

When I wanted to give my tithes, he would say, "What are you tithing for? We're poor! We can't be tithing."

"Sonny," I said, "that's not right. I feel that we have to tithe, if we want God to multiply our money."

So I would tithe anyway. He would really get upset with me when I would do that. When I would get him upset, I had to keep quiet because he had a temper. If I talked back he would hit the wall, and scare me half to death, so I learned when to be quiet.

There were times I wondered if I had made a mistake in marrying Sonny. Then I'd remember how the Lord had spoken to me. Deep inside I was always reminded of that. The Lord didn't force me, He had asked me if I was willing. And I had said yes. Every time I felt like giving up and running, I was reminded of my answer, "Yes."

I got to the point where I felt that I was the most unhappy person in the whole world. He would spend all of his time doing evangelism. Always! If he took a day off he was so tired that he slept all day on the couch. When I could take it no more, I went to Sonny and said, "This life is not normal. You have compassion for everybody but me! What about me? What about the kids?"

He answered, "Look at what God is doing. The devil is using you."

That made me climb the walls all the more. By now we always had several addicts living with us and the church was beginning to grow. That only intensified my frustrations. In the midst of all this activity I was lonely, very lonely.

When Sonny did lose his temper and take his anger out by hitting the walls, it was when no one else was around. When we did argue — most of the time there was somebody there — we had to argue real quiet. It developed some character in both of us. We'd argue and whisper, "You shut up!" and whisper back, "Oh, you be quiet!" because we didn't want to be a stumbling block to all these new Christians who were living in the house.

Most of the time, I wouldn't say anything, but inside I was hurting.

Sonny:

One night a friend of mine and I were taking people home after evening services, when I noticed a sign on a church building: For Rent.

Gless Street Church

The outside of the building needed paint, and the walls were scribbled with obscenities. The next day I went to the church office and talked to the pastor about sharing the building. I told him I was beginning a church and asked if I could rent it Sunday afternoons. He agreed. Julie and I were excited even though the building was in need of much repair. We rejoiced because we had a place in which to meet.

By that time we had between forty and fifty people coming to our living room services. We organized work parties to fix up the church. It took weeks to get the job done because the second week, we saw a drop-off in volunteers.

"That's our biggest problem," I said to Julie. "The follow-through on projects. Sticking with a thing until it's done."

"It's a good thing you're the pastor," Julie laughed. "You'll have to stick with it."

Financially we were in a mess.

My salary was a problem. I agreed to take the very minimum I thought we could exist on, and of course, when the church budget ran low, rent and utilities were paid first, the pastor's salary last. Our salary was only $25 a week. We would have been considerably better off living on a welfare check.

I wondered about my family. Our cupboards were almost always bare, and Julie and our little girls got most of their clothes out of mission boxes. I owned one suit, and it was getting pretty frayed. I pointed out to Julie how well other people I knew were doing. There was Nicky Cruz, and even Harvey the Jew from Brooklyn, who was now traveling as an evangelist.

One night I'd been grumbling, and there was a knock at the door. Outside was Nicky Cruz.

"I'm just traveling through," he said. "I'm speaking at Melodyland tomorrow."

"Man, that's great!" I swallowed my pride and envy and asked him into our tiny kitchen where Julie was fixing dinner. "How about some food?"

Nicky looked great. It was good to have him stop by. He always seemed to enjoy staying with us and sharing whatever we had — even if it meant bunking on the living room sofa.

Later that night, when the dishes were done, and Julie had brought the girls to be hugged and kissed good-night, Nicky looked at me and said, "Man, I wish I could do what you're doing, Sonny."

"You've got to be kidding," I said. "You've got a beautiful wife and children, a great ministry, you travel all over the world..."

"I know," Nicky sighed. "But I don't see my wife and kids as much as I would like to. And don't you remember those lonely motel rooms? They're not like home."

"Yeah, Man," I remembered, and the gratitude suddenly welled up in me. "You're right, I've really got something to thank God for, Nicky," I said.

There were times at the beginning when it was all so difficult. For instance, when I had a singing group scheduled for a service, I never knew whether our congregation was going show up or not. One time just two people showed up and I was so embarrassed. The group said, "When are we gonna start? How we gonna start with nobody here?"

"I guess we will have a street meeting," I answered.

That's how irresponsible our congregation was at the beginning.

I was forever bringing fellows home from the street

for a meal. I'd round up a bunch of addicts and tell them about Jesus Christ, and they would come home with me for supper. Once I brought home ten guys. Julie was in the kitchen and I told her, "Fix enough for another ten guys, Honey."

Julie:

I stared at Sonny without a word, and he went back to the fellows in the living room, expecting me to whip up a meal for ten or twenty on short notice. I enjoyed cooking meals for crowds, even when it's unexpected. I stood in the kitchen crying – we had empty cupboards.

He didn't realize that we had absolutely nothing left to eat except a small amount of pancake mix in the bottom of a box. I measured it — exactly a cup and a half — enough perhaps, for ten or twelve pancakes.

I cried, and then prayed:

"Jesus, what am I going to do? If I tell Sonny there isn't any food, those guys aren't gonna think much of Jesus as a Saviour and Provider. Lord, I'm going to ask You for a miracle. Please do the same thing with my pancake mix that You did with the two loaves of bread and five fishes when You fed five thousand."

Carefully, I poured the mix into a small bowl and added the correct amount of water. Then I began stirring while I looked up at the ceiling and thanked the Lord for the miracle He was performing. I stirred and prayed and stirred and prayed. When I looked down at the bowl, the mix was ready to run over the edges!

Quickly, I reached for a larger bowl and poured the mix into it. Then, I continued to stir and pray. This time it wasn't hard to say, "Thank You, Jesus!" The mix grew in the bowl as I stirred, until it reached the rim again. It looked like plenty for the group Sonny had brought home.

When I put the huge stack of pancakes on the table, I said nothing about the empty cupboard. Not until everyone had eaten and there was still a stack left over on the plate, did I tell them what had happened.

Sonny:

I wondered sometimes why we were always living so close to the poverty line, why we couldn't have a pantry running over with food. Perhaps this was the way God kept us continuously leaning on Him.

Living in the low-income housing projects was really a trying time. But these were the people that God had called us to.

We were poor... We're talking major poverty here. I mean we didn't have any support, we were living on almost nothing. Julie didn't have a washing machine and both Debbie and Doreen were still in diapers. She had to wash the diapers by hand. Julie wanted to get welfare because we qualified. I let her apply for it for one month, and then after that the Lord convicted me and I told her, "I can't preach to these people to get off welfare and us be on it. We've got to trust God. We have to really believe God for everything."

Julie would hang the diapers and clothes out to dry on the clothesline, and if she didn't bring them in before the sun went down they would be stolen by the people in the neighborhood. Crime was rampant in the area. The gangs would mug people right in front of our house. I don't know why, but where we lived was where all the muggings took place.

Early one evening I had walked to the corner liquor store to buy milk and soda, and on my way home I noticed a bunch of guys who looked as though they were planning something. I realized that they were getting ready for a mugging, and I was to be their victim! I usually had a knife slipped in the side of my belt, but that time I had nothing with me. My carrying a knife had really bothered Julie, so I had quit carrying one. (Almost every time I would slip the knife under my belt, she would say, "Sonny, when are you going to quit carrying a knife? Don't you know how to trust God? What would you do if someone did try to mug you? Kill them?")

All of a sudden I saw that one of the guys had a hammer behind his back. I was walking, thinking, *Now what do I do? This is a mugging scene, they're going to approach me any minute. If I try to go across the street they're gonna get me anyway. If I go straight they're still gonna get me.* So it hit me, just go right up to them and witness to them. I didn't have anything to lose. I turned around and walked right up to them, and said, "You know what, I want to tell you that I'm the pastor of the church right down the block."

Automatically I had my hands poised, ready to protect myself. "I used to be a drug addict and mug people. I even used to hit them over the head and take their money. My church is full of of ex-drug addicts who have been saved and delivered by the power of God. I want you to come this Sunday, okay? I'm inviting every one of you to come."

The guy who was going make the first move when I started talking to them, looked at the other guys like, "What do I do?" The other guys didn't know what to do. They were very confused for a moment.

He's dead, but who cares? We did!

I said, "Okay, I'll see you there this Sunday, all right? God bless you," and I kept right on walking.

I walked into the house and said, "Wow, that was a close one."

Julie asked, "What happened?"

I said, "I almost got mugged."

When we first moved into the neighborhood, gangs would steal my car and take it for a joy ride. Finally we began penetrating the area with the gospel. The black gang members started calling me, "Reverend."

"Hey, Reverend. How you doing, Reverend?" Little by little, they began to know me.

The Lord saved some of the guys in the neighborhood and that's when the stealing stopped. They recognized that we really had a genuine concern for them, and started showing us respect. From that point on, things began to change.

There were times when it seemed as though we were fighting the forces of hell all alone. In spite of the difficulties, there was a driving force inside me that would not let me quit. I knew there was a divine call in my life and that God had a definite plan for Julie and I to fulfill.

God knew exactly what I needed. I needed molding. I needed to mature, for the greater things that God had for us.

I was constantly going out to various churches, raising money for the "addict's church." Almost everyone attending our church was on welfare and food stamps.

The people who owned the building on Gless Street decided to sell it. On blind faith we were able to negotiate a deal and buy it for thirteen thousand five hundred dollars. More than ever I would have to go out and raise the money to support the ministry and our new church. I knew how to build a mailing list. I used to go out and preach in the churches and tell them, "I want you to help those who can't help themselves."

Abruptly, God began to impress upon me that these people needed to support the work of God. I had the mind set that they could not actually help themselves. As a matter of fact, that was the philosophy of most everyone I talked to, and they would tell me, "Sonny, you'll never be able to establish a strong church with those kinds of people. They never make good Christians. They need to belong to another church with higher class people, because they'll never grow in a church of their own."

That's when I stopped all promotion, and soliciting support. I started putting the responsibility on them, and told them, "If we're gonna make it, you people who are able bodied have to go to work and get off welfare. It's a do-or-die situation. Either you work and support this ministry, or we'll close the doors. I'm stopping all mailing lists and solicitation, and we're going to trust God to raise you up to support this ministry."

A slow turn-around began to take place from that point on. They gradually began working, got off welfare, and began to tithe.

My salary was now forty-five dollars a week. Julie and I knew that God had called us and knew we had to "pay the price."

It wasn't easy, and Satan fought us every step of the way. There were times when it seemed like we would never make it, especially with these people. It was so frustrating to spend so much of my time getting them integrated into my family and into the church and have them backslide. In the beginning, there was so much of this that our efforts seemed futile.

It was very difficult nurturing them and teaching them to walk with the Lord. When they took on the responsibility of acquiring a job, supporting their families, and giving of themselves to the ministry, backsliding became less of a problem.

When it seemed we were finally making headway in the church and evangelizing the streets, an attack came through my newly-formed church board. When I was away for a few days, they had a secret meeting. They wanted to hire an assistant for me, a man who was politicking to become my assistant.

When I returned from my trip, a deacon came and told me, "Pastor Sonny, we have decided that you need an assistant. We think you should hire him and pay him sixty-five dollars a week."

"You want me to do what?" I was shocked at their suggestion. "Where is the money going to come from? We can hardly keep the doors open as it is. Get with it, Man, and find out what is going on!" I fired back. I was hurt, confused, and angry.

They said no more.

I got so discouraged that I said to Julie, "Can you imagine? Our meager salary is forty-five dollars a week and they want to not only give him more money but they want this slick dude to assist me. I'm gonna quit. This is it. I've had it. I've had enough of this!"

Julie, for the first time, agreed with me. I made an appointment and met with an experienced pastor friend of mine for lunch. While we were having fellowship, I began to share with him the decision that we had made. "We are gonna quit, leave the church, and go back on the field. We have been suffering enough.

"Here we are in this dilapidated church, living below the poverty level and to top it off, the people don't seem to understand what we are going through, and my spirit is hurt," I continued with downcast eyes. "I am losing my vision and fight..."

Suddenly, as I was sharing my feelings with him, the anointing fell on him. **"Sonny, this is not of God.** Don't you believe it. This is not of God. If you leave this church you will regret it for the rest of your life. Sonny, the church won't last six months and you will be in sorrow and anguish. **This is where God is separat-**

ing the men from the boys," he said prophetically.

Without a doubt, I felt that God was speaking to me. I suddenly realized that God had not released me, but I still needed to go forward and confront the situation. The pastor also gave me some good advice, saying, "Go back and love the people, and let God give you wisdom in dealing with the situation."

I went back and told the board, "Why don't you let me work with him for a few months, without pay. Then, if it works out you can begin to pay him."

As soon as they told him that he said, "No way. I'm not gonna work for nothing." They were able to see another side of him that they hadn't seen before. After this, he didn't want anything to do with the church and left.

Soon after that incident, the Lord spoke to me about inviting an evangelist to hold a special series of meetings at the church. I didn't think he would come to a church our size, but I went ahead and called him. I couldn't believe it when he said, "It just happens that my calendar is free for that particular week. It must be God's will. I will be glad to accept your invitation."

He came and we had a great revival. There was a mighty outpouring of the Holy Spirit and over a hundred brand-new souls got saved. That turned the whole church around and spiritually revolutionized us. That revival gave us a spiritual thrust forward like we never had before, and suddenly I felt that we were going to make it. Before that I wasn't sure. It was a day by day experience, trying to build the church. There was doubt in my mind, but after those people got saved, my vision was renewed and Julie and I felt reassured that "Yes, we were going to make it."

It was around that time that Nicky dropped by to visit for a few hours. I was glad for the fellowship with him, it was real refreshing!

"Sonny," Nicky said, "why don't you go with me to the Christian Center Church? I'm sure they would want you to give your testimony. It would be a blessing for you, and David Wilkerson is going to be there."

"Yeah, I responded, "that sounds great!"

When Nicky and I got there, Dave came up to us and said, "I want you two to testify. Nicky, you go first, and then I'll have Sonny speak." Nicky testified, then I got up, and even though I didn't feel inspired, gave a short testimony.

After I testified, Dave said, "I feel that God has told me that we should collect a special offering for Sonny and his ministry."

It was something unexpected. It wasn't even his meeting and he got up and collected an offering. That day I walked in broke and walked out with over $2,000 cash in my pocket.

Once again, God said to me, "Listen, Sonny, you are in My divine will, and I am the One who supplies and the One who provides."

Chapter Eight

Launching Out

A week later I was praising the Lord for what He was doing, when I realized how close I had come to quitting. I truly would have regretted it for the rest of my life. Satan fights the hardest when we are on the brink of a miracle and a spiritual breakthrough.

Thank God for my preacher friend who had the courage to prophesy a hard word to me.

We lived in the projects for three and a half-years. Many wonderful things happened there. We were crowding the people into that small apartment like sardines. We weren't supposed to have anyone living there except our family. We knew we had to have a larger house, but our faith wasn't quite that big. The government changed that quickly, when we were told to get rid of the other "live-ins" or get out. We decided to move.

We were paying thirty-two dollars a month in the

project. We found a big, three-story house we could rent for $125 a month, which would require a real leap of faith. At that time, the offerings were still rather small. However, we felt that this was the place God had for us, so we rented it.

Victory Home

Julie and I were standing in the living room, praising God for this new home, when I told her, "Julie, it's time we had some privacy as a family. We will keep all of the first floor for us, put the women on the second floor, and the men on the third floor. Honey, things will be different here. You will see."

A lot of the men who were staying at the house were married. Julie took on the responsibility of ministering to their wives, who were mostly burned out and bitter. They had been lied to and abused, so they were very skeptical when they saw their husbands saved. They couldn't believe that God had really changed them. When they would see their husbands in church, praising the Lord, they would say, "Oh, now that you're all cleaned up, and doing so good, why don't you get a job and start supporting us? Why don't you come home and see what you can do for us now?"

We knew, however, that they needed more of the Word and faith before they could leave the home. Julie would take our car and pick wives up for church, because a lot of them didn't have cars. Anybody who had a car made four or five trips to pick up people and bring them to church.

Julie:

One Sunday, I was running a bit late. This particular woman had a habit of screaming at me every time I showed up. I went to her door and she started right off yelling at me, "Look at you, you are late, and now I have to walk into church in front of everyone!" She had some of her baby things in her arms and screamed, "Carry this!"

I took them as the woman blew cigarette smoke in my face. I was thinking: You know wh*at? I don't have to do this. You can just stay home! I'm just not going to* *take it anymore.* As we got in the car, this woman was still sounding off.

I thought, I w*onder what these other girls are thinking while she's screaming at me? They're probably losing respect for me because I'm not standing up for myself. These girls are from the street.*

Right when I was ready to lose my composure and explode, one of the girls who was sitting in the front seat turned around to the girl who was screaming at me and said, "You know what, this is the last time I ever want to hear you talk to Julie like that. Do you hear me? If you do, you're gonna have to mess with me. And that goes for all of you."

The Lord had raised her up to protect me. Then she finished, "I don't ever want to hear any more disrespect for her. God has sent her to us, and we should be grateful for her."

That's the type of women we had. Many of them had even used drugs with their husbands, and some of them had stooped so low that they sold their bodies to support both their habits, thus losing all self-respect.

Sonny:

When we took a man in off the streets or from prison, they stayed with us for about nine months. We would let them go home for the weekend or on passes after several months at the house.

Every Tuesday night we would ask the wives and children to come over to our house. The wives could come, talk to their husbands, and bring their children. We had a packed out house, and sometimes major fights would break out. Tuesday nights were supposed to be a happy time, but sometimes it would turn into a nightmare. One Tuesday night, Mike and his wife got in a fist fight. She was very aggravated and came at him saying, "You've been here too long. Why don't you come home and start taking care of your family?"

The wives expected them to come home to face responsibilities before they were ready. Then when they fell on their faces, they wanted them to receive help from us again.

Their stay with us was voluntary, but if they did decide to stay they had to obey the rules. They had to get approval to leave the house and they had to go with someone else. They lived in a controlled environment.

Before we realized it, word on the street was that there was a home where lives were being changed. It got so crowded that when we walked in at night, we were stepping over bodies all the way to the bedrooms, because people were everywhere. It was wall to wall people. We were housing about fifty addicts.

In the home, Julie would get up real early, about six, and make everybody breakfast. Most of the time it was oatmeal. If we got someone in who knew how to cook, she would put him to making a dinner. We always had to be careful, because the little food that we did have, had to stretch.

One of the men who was living with us was a guy named Freddie Hernandez. He had a brother named Rudy, who was a young man who was destined to live out his life in prison or die on the streets.

He was one of eleven children. Freddie had come into our home and after getting gloriously converted, wanted to reach his entire family. He invited Rudy, who was a short, young man, with a big smile, but very few teeth, to come to church. After one church service, I went up to him and asked, "What did you think of the services?"

He gave me a stern look and said, "I don't believe in God, I only came to see my brother, Freddie."

I could tell he was down and out and hungry, so I said, "Why don't you drop over to our house and have lunch with us?"

He replied, "No, I don't think so."

I put my hand on his shoulder and told him, "Our house is open to you anytime."

He looked at me with a puzzled look and asked, "Even if I don't believe in God – any god?"

I looked at him straight in the eye and said, "Yes, God even loves atheists!"

To my surprise, Rudy joined us for lunch that day and miraculously decided to stay for a few days. He was a true atheist and tried my patience over and over again. He'd refute everything I'd say and when he saw that I was getting angry, he'd laugh viciously in my face.

Rudy was a real challenge to me. He watched my every step and latched on to every word I spoke. He contradicted me in front of the guys and soon our Bible studies became debates. One night, Julie and I were getting ready for bed when through our paper-thin walls, we could hear him arguing with the guys upstairs. I turned to Julie and said, "This is it! I'm throwing him out! I give up on that heathen."

I put my pants on and stormed up the stairs. I yelled at him, "Rudy, I've had enough of this arguing and debating. Do you want God? Say 'yes', or 'no.' If it's 'no,' you can just leave. If it's 'yes,' I'll continue with God's help to lead you and teach you. I'll do everything in my power to see you become a man of God."

I stood there waiting for his response. I could see drops of sweat gathering in his forehead. As he hung his head, the Lord filled me with such love and compassion for him.

He looked up at me and said, "Sonny, I've been here now for several weeks and I know I've given you and Julie a hard time, but you have to understand, I've never really been accepted by anyone before. I don't remember anyone ever telling me they loved me, or showing me any love. Not my brothers; my mother; no one, ever. I don't know how to respond — how do I receive love? Here you are showing me all this love, taking me into your own home, when you don't even know me. Sonny, give me time, you may not see anything happening in me, but it is. I think I'm getting ready to accept your Jesus for myself."

We all gathered around him and began to pray. It was a joy for me to hear him cry out for forgiveness. "Lord, forgive me for being so rebellious. I believe You are the Son of God and died for me. Come into my heart, Lord Jesus. Cleanse me of all my sin."

The glory of God's presence filled the room. We all fell to our knees and for the first time, I saw Rudy get on his knees and weep before God.

The next few months I kept him close to me, sharing my heart to him. One day, he asked me, "Pastor Sonny, what is discipleship?"

"Rudy, it's not so much what we read in books, what we are referring to in discipleship is a transferring of one's faith in Christ to another. We practice, we know, and we understand some of the processes, but we do not fully comprehend this tremendous principle. It is a powerful principle of the kingdom of God and a spiritual happening. Whatever we are as a person or a leader, we impart to others."

He slowly asked, "How do I become a disciple?"

"Rudy," I said, "you are already a disciple, without realizing it. Discipleship is an empowering of soul and spirit. A disciple is a learner. If we associate long enough with someone who loves God, and is on fire, believe me, we are going to catch it."

Rudy began to catch it. He learned how to pray and

speak with God. He began to study the Word of God and the Lord opened up his understanding. He had a burning desire to learn so he, too, could teach others. I could tell he was going to grow and be one of God's key men in the future of Victory Outreach.

The church services continued growing in number, and God began moving in a new way. I would start preaching a regular sermon, and then the Spirit of God would come upon me, and I would begin to prophesy, as I felt the anointing. "God is going to raise up many of you. He's going to raise up pastors and evangelists, and missionaries, and He will send you all over the world. God will raise you up, as He raised up this ministry for that purpose." After I would finish and the Spirit would lift, I would look at them in disbelief. I would see their faces, and see the reality of who was sitting in the congregation. There were guys with big moustaches, tattoos, and scarred faces, seemed to be impossible cases. Then there were the girls whose very appearance portrayed the hard life they had led. Then I would think, *What in the world made me say that?*

When I would leave the platform I would ask Julie, "Did you hear what I said?"

"Yeah, you sure were talking big," she would answer with a smile.

"I don't know what in the world I was thinking when I said that. I gotta be careful. I don't want to exaggerate, but I know that it was God who spoke through me."

Through natural eyes, it was very difficult to be able to really see that out of that group of people, God would be able to do anything big. At the time, even though I was following God, and was being obedient to His calling, it was difficult for me to believe that God was able to raise up a powerful ministry through those men and women. Most were graduates from San Quentin Prison, and various other institutions. These people, for the most part, had hardly ever worked before in their lives — impossible cases. Most of them had failed at just about everything. But God continued to say that He was going to raise many of them up, and they would go, not only all over California, but imagine this: He said, "All over the world."

I didn't want to mislead the congregation, but there I'd go again, prophesying, "And many of you, God is gonna raise up, and you're gonna be pastors and evangelists, and tremendous leaders that He will raise up to use all over the world."

Then, after the anointing would lift I would say, "There, Julie, I said it again."

"You sound so convincing, I'm beginning to believe it myself," Julie responded.

Slowly, but surely something began to happen within the lives of these men. One of the most impossible men, that I would never have thought would amount to anything, came up to me. He had been in San Quentin Prison, and had a gangster mentality. He was a short guy, and talked through the side of his mouth, like James Cagney. "You know what, Pastor," he said to me. "I've been hearing everything you said, and I want you to know that I am that guy you were talking about. God has called me, and I believe He is sending me out. I'm going to be the first one God will send out from Victory Outreach to establish a work for Him."

When he said that I looked at him, and I thought, *Oh, here we go again!* I didn't believe him. I kind of pacified him and said, "That is fine, Gilbert, if it's God's will it will happen. Just go back to your seat and take it easy. Let's pray about it."

Something was born inside of Gilbert that day. He got hold of that word from God, so much that he went out, without even being sent! He was still attending the church, and started having a Bible study in his neighborhood. That Bible study grew, and in a short time he had over a hundred brand-new souls. He kept telling me I had to come see what was happening.

One Sunday morning, before our own service, I went over there to see what he was doing. They were already meeting in a church building. I arrived early and as I walked up to the church, I could hear what sounded like prayer coming from the sanctuary. Gilbert walked out to meet me. "Pastor Sonny, I'm so glad you came. The guys and girls are so excited to meet you."

When I walked in, I saw teenage gang girls on their knees before God. As I looked around, I could see young men with their tattooed arms raised telling God how much they loved Him. They had tears streaming down their faces; God's presence was there. Gilbert said, "Pastor Sonny, we're following the same pattern as the parent church. I tell them to come one hour before service begins so they can have a time alone with God."

That's the first time I heard the term, "the parent church."

First baby church. Gilbert and Mary Garavito.

Gilbert and I joined in on the prayer meeting. As I prayed, I thanked the Lord for the miracle birth of our first baby church in Pico Rivera. The next Sunday I announced that we were going to be launching out our very first pastor that God had raised up. All of our people were excited, because they knew Gilbert. The following Sunday, our church was packed out. Gilbert brought the hundred young people that God already had given him.

I saw the blessing of God upon him and his ministry. We installed him as the very first Victory Outreach pastor. Step by step I could see God was unfolding His plan.

The other men were watching and saying, "Do you mean to tell me they're going to launch this guy out? He came up from the ranks."

About six months later, on a Saturday night, after Gilbert had prepared his message for Sunday morning, he went to bed, and never woke up. His wife called me that Sunday morning crying, "Pastor Sonny, you'll never believe it. Gilbert passed away in the middle of the night. When I woke up, he was gone. Please, can somebody come and take care of the service?" We had a beautiful funeral for him, and Julie and I mourned with his lovely wife.

Gilbert's sudden death had a sad, but powerful effect on many of the men. They started coming up to me telling me they had the same burden. One of those men was Philip LaCrue, who was a handsome, young man. He had been raised in a very religious home, but he started using drugs at an early age. By the time he was fifteen years old, he had become a hard-core heroin addict...one of the walking dead. When this boy came to us, he was skin and bones. He had come straight from jail and I had doubts that he would make it. He was never still, he seemed hyper all the time. To my surprise, Philip began to grasp the message of the gospel and as I was preaching, I could see him sit eagerly in the front row so he could absorb all that was said.

Now there he stood, years later, saying, "Pastor, I am the one God has called to take Gilbert's place."

We agreed and sent him to Pico Rivera.

Julie:

By now we had three kids. We had added Sonny, Jr.

During those years, although God was doing great things in the men and women who were living with us, the pressures of the close-knit family of fifty were building up within me. We lived together, ate together, slept and shared devotions, all within the same house. I longed for a romantic walk with Sonny, a family picnic, and some attention. We could feel the oppression of Satan's forces at work because some of them came to us possessed. Almost without exception, everyone we took in came with either a severe case of depression, had served a long prison term, or had a life-controlling habit. In spite of all the turmoil going on within me, I somehow managed to continue to give to those in need.

Sonny:

Julie would say to me, "Sonny, I can't take it anymore. I feel as if I don't even have a husband. You're always gone. I don't want to be here anymore." When she would start to express herself, I would be so physically tired that I didn't want to hear her, so I'd walk out and leave.

As a result, she got real sick and depressed. I think all her hidden bitterness was too much and she ended up going to the hospital for a week. By then, Julie and I had grown apart because I was so busy doing my own thing with the ministry. I had a good heart, but the wrong concepts. I put God first, the ministry second, and Julie and the kids last.

Just think, Julie was in the hospital a week and I only visited her once. She was real sick, with tubes in her and everything. The poison had gotten into her entire system. She began to pray to God, "Why don't You just take me. I'm just a stumbling block. Sonny keeps telling me how the devil is using me, I just want to be with You. I want to die."

She had just given birth to Sonny, Jr., and she hardly had anyone to talk to. The people that were close to her were new converts and she couldn't tell them her problems. She did talk to some pastor's wives, and they told her, "Leave! You're not supposed to live like that with all those addicts!"

She cried out to the Lord, "Just take me, I should go,

I don't want to be here anymore."

That's the way she was feeling. It was foolish, I know, but she prayed like that anyway. When she got out of the hospital, she wore a size one dress. Just skin and bones. It was severe, severe depression. I can identify it now. But at that time, I was too young and I didn't understand all the things that she was going through.

I started realizing that I was so involved in the building of the ministry that I actually neglected Julie, and the children. My philosophy was that she was to be quiet and submitted. After all, I was doing the work of God, and that had to be first. I felt that I needed to give my all, one hundred percent to the ministry, and that's exactly what I did.

I found myself not only being the pastor to the guys that were coming in, but I was also their friend. I still had the habit of hanging out with the boys. I would go out with them, maybe eat, talk, and fellowship and come home to have a prayer meeting that sometimes lasted until two or three o'clock in the morning. I would wake up early the next day and have prayer and Bible study with the guys again. Even when Julie was having Sonny, Jr., I took her and dropped her off at the hospital, saying, "Okay, go ahead and have the baby, and I'll come by and see you later." I was very insensitive towards her. *After all*, I thought, *she's my partner. She has to rough it. Toughen up. What's she whining about? We're in the ministry, she's gotta be able to put up with whatever I'm putting up with. I've dedicated my life to God, and instead of hindering me and complaining, she should be praying and seeking God.* That was my mentality at the time.

I had a temper, a real rough temper. God began to take that away, little by little. It was a process of maturity that was taking place in my life. There were moments when I felt that we probably weren't going to make it as a husband and wife, because we got into some heavy arguments. I would always blame her saying, "Julie, you are a stumbling block, and you're vulnerable to the devil. Instead of being aware of the tactics of the enemy, you are opening yourself up to the devil, and he is using you." I looked at her as if she was weak for wanting lots of attention. *Why does she need all this attention? She should just dedicate herself, and sacrifice, like everyone else. Look what Jesus did, He sacrificed himself. Can't she sacrifice herself?* It was really a horrible time for her. I was sincere in what I was doing. I was sincerely wrong. I thought that what I was doing was right, and if I had to sacrifice my wife and children for the ministry, then I was willing to sacrifice them.

Julie:

We decided we needed to take some time off and went to Mexico for a few days. Several pastors heard Sonny was coming and asked him to hold a crusade; I was still very weak and sick and stayed in the background. The open air meeting was packed. I attended the meeting but stayed off the stage.

After Sonny preached and gave the altar call, I asked for him to come to me, because I wasn't feeling well. He walked over to me and said, "What's wrong?"

"I don't feel good," I faintly whispered. "Sonny, I'm going!" and collapsed. I was told that Sonny picked me up and carried me to a hut close by and he laid me on the bed. During that time I had an out-of-the-body experience. I knew I was going somewhere, as I could feel my body speeding like a projected rocket toward heaven.

I thought, *Oh, my God, I've died. My prayer has been answered!*

Then I realized how foolish I had been and said, "God, you have answered me. You are taking me. What about my children? What about the ministry? What about all these things that I haven't accomplished for You yet? I'm sorry, I'll never pray like that again. Please forgive me. Forgive me. I want to go back and raise my children and be a good wife for Sonny."

I realized that at any moment I could be in the presence of God. I knew if I saw God I wouldn't be able to come back. When I came to, Sonny was shaking and slapping me, trying to revive me.

I cried, "I'm back, I'm back." I was so happy. I hugged Sonny and I thanked the Lord for another chance.

The relationship and circumstances in our marriage

didn't change right away, but major transitions began to take place in me. I was so grateful to be a mother and my desires were renewed to mother my children.

I also wanted to be a positive factor in Sonny's life. I stopped nagging him, and started being a blessing to him. I knew that I had to support him and wait for him to change.

I went back to what I knew best...prayer. I began to take my eyes off the difficult circumstances and put my faith in God. The Lord began to restore my shattered emotions from that point on.

Chapter Nine

Treasures Out of Darkness

There were many moments of discouragement in the ministry. God didn't show me the whole picture, and many times I would ask, "What's going to happen in the future?"

There were times where I felt like everything was gonna fall apart, or we weren't going any further and again, I would need reassurance from God. My faith at times would waiver.

I was in that state of mind when I was invited to speak at a conference. "Lord," I said, "You have to speak to me today. I need to have confirmation, again. I need to hear from You, I need to have a word from You."

I went to the meeting, and the first speaker didn't really have anything to say that was for me. Then I spoke. After me Dick Mills spoke, and even his message wasn't for me. When he was just about to finish. I was thinking, *Lord, You still have to speak to me.*

Dick Mills then said, "I can't turn it over to the pastor until I give this word. Sonny, I have a word for you from the Lord. Stand up right now."

I stood up, and he gave me this Scripture found in Isaiah 45:2-3:

"I will go before thee, and make the crooked places straight: I will break in pieces the gates of brass, and cut in sunder the bars of iron: And I will give thee the treasures of darkness, and hidden riches of secret places, that thou mayest know that I, the Lord, which call thee by thy name, am the God of Israel."

Then he said, "Write these verses down, Sonny. Read them again and again. These are words from the Almighty God sent special delivery just for you."

As I got hold of that Scripture, and I made it mine. I thought, *This is it, this is what I needed. I have heard from God.* By the time I got home it was late. I walked into the bedroom. Julie was waiting up for me. She knew how troubled I had been and that I needed the Lord to reassure me. "How did it go, Sonny?" she asked.

I took the little paper with my promise written on it out of my pocket, gave it to her, and said, "Here, read this," she took the paper, unfolded it, and held it closer to the lamp on the night stand.

After she read it, she looked at me and said, "Sonny, this promise is so beautiful."

I went around the bed and knelt next to her. She turned to Isaiah and began to read it aloud from the Bible. She then handed the paper back to me and I read it aloud:

"And I will go before thee and make the crooked places straight..."

"Julie, do you see what He's saying? He's going to go before us. He is going to straighten things."

I continued reading, "I will break in pieces the gates of brass and cut asunder the bars of iron."

Julie said, "I think this means the prisons, Sonny, He's going to penetrate and give us a revival with hard-core prisoners."

With tears streaming down her face, she read, "And I will give you treasures out of darkness and hidden riches in secret places."

Suddenly, I got a knot in my throat and tears came to my eyes also, as I realized how the Lord himself was reminding me that He was going to use us to not only reach the drug addicts, gang members, and prostitutes, but that He was going to make "treasures" out of them. He had "treasures" and "hidden riches" in secret places. This reminded me of the inner cities of the world, those hiding in shame in dark alleys were going to be redeemed by the blood of Jesus. They then would be used to reach others, causing a revival to break out in the darkest, most sinful demon-controlled places. God himself, was going to do it. It was a promise given to us so that Julie and I would always remember that He who called us by name is God, Jehovah.

From that moment on those verses have become the foundational Scripture and promise of Victory Outreach Ministries. Everywhere you go within the ministry, you see "Treasures Out of Darkness." Not only has it become my promise to cling to, but in moments of discouragement the entire ministry gets hold of that Scripture. It is even the name of our television program, *Treasures Out of Darkness,* and now the name of this book.

God is faithful, and has given us thousands of "Treasures Out of Darkness," who were into every conceivable sin one could imagine, those impossible cases that were in total darkness. When they were in darkness they were unproductive, nobody wanted them. Sadly, the reality is that many pastors don't want people like that in their congregations, because they feel that they are going to lose the "good" people. This is why many say to these people, "Go to the Victory Outreach Church." Pastors bring us the prostitutes, saying, "These are not our ministry, we don't have that anointing. Here, take them."

Julie:

After about seven years of sharing our home with people in need, Sonny and I felt we needed to be alone. We needed to move from the rehabilitation home, at least for a short time. My mom and dad felt a call into the ministry and began to run the rehabilitation home. They gave themselves wholeheartedly to the work and loved the men and women just like we did.

Sonny and I found the house of our dreams. When one lives in a rehab situation for years on end, anything is a dream. We had a lease on it with an option to buy. We had only been there a little over three months when one night, I felt impressed that I should close the door to the living room. I never closed that door. When I closed it, it didn't shut tight, and I walked away. Then I heard a voice that clearly told me to go back and close it tight. I went back and made sure that it was tight. I didn't know why I was doing that. I just obeyed the voice and went to bed.

In the middle of the night, about three o'clock, I was awakened by some crackling noises, and I thought at the time it was raining. It got a little bit louder, so I shook Sonny and said, "Sonny, I hear something strange, you had better get up and check it."

"It's nothing, just go back to sleep. I'm not going to get up. If you want to know what it is, you get up," he said.

I went to the living room door, and when I took hold of the knob it was real hot. I opened it, and saw the flames. That door closed off the rest of the house; the kid's bedroom was opposite ours.

"Sonny!" I screamed. "There's a fire! Get up!" By then the wiring had burned and we had no electricity. It was too dark to see anything. Again, I screamed, "Sonny, you better hurry up, we have to do something."

"I can't find my pants, I can't find my pants!" he yelled.

"Get the kids out! Get the kids out!"

"I can't go without my pants on."

"Forget your pants," I pleaded. "Go out in your boxers."

He wouldn't do anything until he found his pants.

"The kids are gonna die!" I screamed.

We got the kids out through the back of the house. Sonny got a garden hose, and tried to put out the fire, which by now was burning out of control. The children and I sat across the street on the curb, and watched the house burn. It seemed like forever until the fire department got there, but I'm sure they were there right away. I wasn't thinking about the things that were burning. I didn't have that many possessions. I was grateful that my children were safe. I started realizing while I was sitting there, how the Lord was the One who had told me to close the door, and how He guided me that night or we all would have died.

People heard about what happened to us, and many good friends surrounded us and began to give us clothes, furniture, and appliances.

All of the living room, kitchen, and the walls of the bedrooms had burned. Everything we had was burned. We were left with nothing, but were grateful that God had spared our lives. A few weeks after the fire we found another little house and purchased it.

Sonny with Debbie, Doreen, Sonny Boy & Georgina.

Sonny:

In the very beginning of our ministry on Gless Street, our vision was to reach East L.A. That was the length and width of our vision. I was always looking for ways of reaching the gang members and drug addicts for Christ. Our methods were very unique. (We could hardly walk up to them and just say, "Come to church.") We had to go out and have different street crusades and rallies.

Our slogan for Victory Outreach then was, "Let's win East L.A. for Jesus." As I said before, our whole burden was to saturate East L.A. with the gospel of Jesus Christ. East L.A. is an area that is primarily Hispanic and black, and where there are many gangs. Many of these gangs have been in existence for over eighty years. These territorial neighborhoods go back three and four generations. They were willing to die to protect a few blocks. They were loyal to their "hood."

The burden to reach the gangs began to burn within my spirit. I prayed and prayed, asking the Lord, "Please, God, show me how to reach the gangs for You. These kids are being killed every day without You."

In a few days the answer came, "Hold a big gang rally in a public auditorium!"

I knew that the Lord had spoken clearly to me to have a rally. I also wanted the confirmation of our staff. I called them together and told them what I thought God wanted. That was to hold, to my knowledge, the first gang rally in our area, under the auspices of a church. Every one of the staff thought it was a good idea, and almost in unison said, "Man, let's go for it!"

I said to them, "I think it would be a good idea to ask Nicky Cruz to come and speak. He's so well-known, and he's an ex-gang member. Let's all pray that he will say yes. I also think it would be a good idea if we would try to get the Belvedere Junior High School Auditorium, and get other pastors to join in with us."

Then we discussed the various means of how we were actually going to get the gang members to come. One said, "Well, we have to make sure that we declare it all neutral territory, so there won't be any fighting, or shooting, or anything like that."

We printed brochures by the thousands, inviting all of the gangs to come to Belvedere Junior High, which we declared neutral ground, to hear Nicky Cruz. We hit the streets and started inviting the gang members to the meeting. I decided I would take it on myself to visit the pastors and invite them to join us, but I was told, "A gang rally? We've never heard of such a thing! What if there's a fight? What if somebody gets killed? Anybody in his right mind would be afraid to go to a meeting like that."

Others would say, "Sonny, it's a good idea, but we just don't want to be involved."

We went ahead because we really felt that it was God, and started blanketing the meeting in prayer. We told the members of the various gangs before they came, not to be carrying guns, knives, or any type of weapon, because we didn't want any trouble. We even decided that we would provide transportation for those wanting to come who didn't have a way.

The night of the rally, the auditorium was completely packed. Nicky shared, and gave his testimony, then he gave a beautiful altar call. There were a few hundred of the gang members that came forward and gave their lives to Jesus.

We had done so much advertising that the media was there, and they wrote it up. One of the headlines said, **Gang Rally a Success – Many Respond to the Call of God.** There was also a number of the pastors I invited who came, just to check it out and to see what was actually going on. The next night, after all the publicity, the auditorium was so packed out that we had to turn people away.

That night I was so thrilled that I told the people there, "Be sure to look for the date next month, because we are going to have another rally. The next time, it's going to be in a larger auditorium, at the East Los Angeles College."

It seated two thousand people, where Belvedere only seated nine hundred.

The next month, the gang rally in the larger auditorium was also packed out. This time we not only had Nicky Cruz, but we had also invited Pat Boone. On

Friday night, when Pat came out onto the stage, they started yelling, "Hey, Pat, where's your white shoes?"

Sonny, Pat Boone, and Nicky Cruz

He really hammed it up and showed them his white shoes. They then started chanting, "Where's your daughter, Debbie? We wanna meet Debbie!" Believe me, it was quite a rowdy audience, but Pat and Nicky handled the situation well.

As the gang members walked into the auditorium, many of them were carrying weapons. Some were wearing them on or under their belts; others in their jacket pockets. Those minutes before the rally began were very tense. Everyone was looking around, watching their backs. About two hundred of our ex-gang members sat among the audience as "undercover" prayer agents.

We could hear and feel the pulsating heartbeat of evil. It was everywhere. There was a constant rumbling that sounded like any second it would blow up or expose itself. We prayed more intently the power of the blood of Jesus over the crowd. The Holy Spirit soon calmed their hearts.

We had a huge choir sing that night, and following Pat, Nicky came and again gave his testimony, and the altar call. We were overwhelmed at the response. As we looked and experienced what God was doing, we wept. Every kind of fallen humanity that you could ever imagine was streaming forward to a better life – eternal life with Jesus. Murders, prostitutes, dopers, bikers, alcoholics, the forgotten, the lonely, forsaken souls were becoming God's new **Treasures Out of Darkness.**

From that meeting we established what was called "Gangs For Christ." That was the beginning of a whole, new ministry in dealing with these little gangsters and their neighborhood ghettos. We knew that if we were going to have continued success we had to disciple these kids and people who were finding Jesus. Since we had such success with the gang rally, I said to the staff, "Because we had such success with the gangs, why don't we have a junkie rally?" They looked at me with their eyes wide open, and one said, "Pastor Sonny, nobody's ever held a junkie rally. Maybe we're going a little too far."

I responded simply, "If we could get the gangs to come, surely we can do the same thing with the drug addicts. They need freedom in Jesus Christ just as anybody else."

In faith believing, we invited the drug addicts to come in, and again the auditorium was packed out. This time we invited Art Linkletter to come and to share with the group. You might say, "Art Linkletter? What would he have to do with drug addicts?" A lot. He had a daughter who had a bad trip, and obviously thinking she could fly, jumped out a window and killed herself.

Almost everyone in the auditorium was from the streets. After Art Linkletter testified, which was absolutely electrifying, I gave an altar call, and again, literally hundreds came forward and gave their lives to Christ.

It became very obvious that we were experiencing a tremendous breakthrough. We were doing what I would call radical evangelism. God had given us the burden, and we were simply obeying the methods that the Lord had laid in our hearts. To everyone's amazement, at these rallies, there were no disorderly episodes. Nobody was shot. There were no real fights that took place. Everything turned out to be a success, under the protection of the Spirit of God.

Soon we had the television, the newspapers, all kinds of media there covering these amazing rallies. It became obvious to us that the East L.A. for Jesus vision was becoming a reality. Even though our church had not reached thousands in numbers it was constantly growing.

Many who gave their lives to the Lord at the crusades came to check out our church on Gless Street. One of the young men was Saul Garcia. He had served fourteen months in the hot jungles of the Vietnam War.

After the crusade he had received a flyer with our church address on it and decided to check it out. When he came in, he couldn't believe this little church on Gless Street was responsible for the large crusade with thousands of people, especially with Pat Boone and Nicky Cruz. I remember the first time he and his wife came to the church. Saul's long hair was in a ponytail and he had a miserable expression on his face. Stella, his wife, walked in wearing a mini-skirt and high heels. She had a big smile and clung to his arm throughout the church service. Every time I looked over at them, it didn't seem as if they were listening.

When the service was over, I greeted them. "God bless you," I said. He didn't respond, so I repeated it, "God bless you." I thought he didn't hear me. His wife smiled and said a courteous, "Hello."

Is he angry? I thought.

Suddenly, without warning, he began to cry. Between sobs, he managed to say, "I have finally found what I am looking for!" and began sharing his Vietnam experiences with us.

"Pastor, when I was in Vietnam, I encountered the enemy almost daily, since I was in the heat of the battle. I took shelter in a little bamboo shack. Bullets were flying everywhere and literally shattering the shack down on top of me. When I realized that I was going to die, I desperately cried out to the Lord saying, 'God, if You get me out of this, I'll serve You the rest of my life.'"

Saul and Stella continued to attend church faithfully. As time went on and I drew close to him, I realized what a negative person he was. Every time I'd gather the guys around me with an idea, he'd be analyzing how it couldn't be done. It got so I would purposely avoid him. Little did I know, God had Saul in His hands and that this negative young man with his hair in a ponytail would grow to be a great man of God, and be one of my right hand men.

We had held church services on Gless Street for about five years when we outgrew the facilities. Very soon, there was another building that opened up for us. It was about two miles away on St. Louis Street. The building would accommodate close to five hundred people and it was right next to the police station.

It was a mighty step of faith, but we went ahead and purchased it for $55,000. We had to come up with the down payment and a Christian foundation loaned us the rest at a very low interest rate. We then turned the building on Gless Street into a rehab center. We were maximizing the use of all the facilities.

We put Rudy Hernandez, my ex-atheist disciple, in charge. God had raised him up and everyone in the rehab home and in the church could see an anointing on his life.

Even though God was pouring out his blessings in East L.A., I still had a heartbeat for New York City. Every summer after my conversion, Julie and I would go back to visit my parents and my "old stomping grounds."

I remember many times walking the streets with Julie. While we were away in California, I'd forgotten how dirty New York was, the soot on the buildings, the rat-infested empty store fronts, the sidewalks crowded with winos and junkies. Even with all this filth, I'd take a deep breath and say to Julie, "Man, I love New York!" Julie knew how I felt.

I'd talk to people on the streets and my heart would fill with compassion. I'd wonder why the Lord hadn't permitted me to be the one to bring the gospel to my own city.

At St. Louis Street, the work began to grow even more. Wonderful things were taking place because we had more facilities for the children, and there was more room in the church auditorium.

Our teams went out daily two by two, evangelizing our "Jerusalem." The Lord gave us a precious couple named Mando and Arline, who lived only a few blocks from the church. When Arline was five years old, her mother and father had a brutal fight. She heard her dad say he was leaving and never coming back. As he slammed the door behind him, she saw her mother go to the window ledge of her high-rise apartment, threatening to jump.

A few neighbors and on-lookers on the street yelled to her, "Becky, don't do it." Someone called the fire department. Quivering and trembling inside the apartment was little Arline.

"I don't want to live anymore," Becky screamed.

Arline cried desperately, "Mama, don't jump. Mama, please don't jump!"

Her mom looked back at Arline and jumped. Arline ran to the window ledge and looked down – her mom was lying on the pavement...people were screaming and crying. Her back was broken, but miraculously, she didn't die. Arline was taken to a children's home and was made a ward of the court. After four years, the authorities released her once again to her mother.

Her mom had become a drug addict and was continually suicidal. Once again, Arline had to watch her mother's death-defying dramas. By the tender age of nine, she had experienced seeing her mother trying to overdose on pills, slice her wrists, and throw herself in front of automobiles, all in an effort to end her life.

After attempting to slice her throat in front of her children, the authorities finally put her mother in a mental hospital. After that horrifying incident, Arline went to live with relatives. When she was seventeen, she met Mando. After a three-month courtship, they were married.

He was a heroin addict and had used drugs for years. Mando's father had been in prison for twenty years for murder. Their marriage would suffer many years of separation because of his life of jails and using drugs.

When I first met Mando and Arline, I had heard of their conversion a few days earlier and was anxious, as their pastor, to meet and welcome them into the family. It was Christmas time and the church was having our annual Christmas party. Mando still had a hard appearance, with his big moustache and rugged expressions, but as we began to converse, I could see he and his precious wife, Arline, had experienced a genuine encounter with Christ. Their faces shone with an inward light as they tried to express their new-found joy.

Mando had a difficult time expressing himself, but the tears that flowed down his face spoke more than a thousand words. He said, "Pastor Sonny, I want you to know Arline and I are here to stay and that we are willing to do anything to help our church. We've prayed and we want to offer ourselves to clean the church. Would that be okay?" he asked.

I was touched by their sincerity and said, "Yes, of course."

Daily, they vacuumed the sanctuary and mopped and cleaned the restrooms. After a few months, they were not only doing janitorial duties, but they became active in street evangelism.

Julie became a second mother to Arline and I took Mando under my wing. I could see something special happening in their lives. The Lord had given this humble couple a special grace and anointing.

One day, Julie and I were sitting down at dinner with Debbie, Doreen, and Sonny, Jr. Julie turned to me and said, "It's so good that we finally have disciples that have captured your heart and have taken over the responsibility of the rehabilitation homes."

"I agree, Julie. I went to visit Rudy today and he is not just baby-sitting the men, but he is discipling those in his care. He's been teaching them how to pray and lean on God," I said.

Julie and I continued talking about how the Lord was raising up leadership, so I had more time to be with my family. I was even learning how to repair things around the house. With the help of some of the men I had painted our new home inside and out.

We had lived in our new home for six months, when two properties opened up to the ministry. One was a 200-acre ranch in Victorville, California, that we could buy for $70,000. So we went ahead and made that purchase. The other piece of property was a six-acre dream. There were tennis courts, a place for horses, swimming pool, and an ideal, lodge-type house that was huge. One could house, very comfortably, fifty, to sixty people in the house. It was Spanish architecture with beautiful, thick, white walls and tile floors. The central living room had chandeliers and a floor to ceiling fireplace. In the center of the grounds was a tile fish pond with a fountain.

The people who rented it were moving out, so they told us who was the owner. I went and talked with him and he was willing to rent it to us.

I felt that the only way that we could really afford that was for us to also live on the property as well. There was another family that was also willing to move to the property with us.

Because the property was twenty-five minutes away from the church, some of the people couldn't understand why we wanted to acquire the property. Some started to criticize and say, "It's too much money. We can't afford that and the church, too." They started using a lot of logic.

Our children were now eight, six, and four, and Julie was pregnant. She gathered the children around her and told them what was happening and they prayed.

I felt definitely in my spirit that the property in West Covina was for us and we needed to get hold of it. I felt so strongly about it I said to our leaders in a meeting,

"Even if the church can't afford it, Julie and I will move to the property and lease it ourselves."

I told Julie, "If we don't claim this land, we may lose it. This is a beautiful piece of property. You don't have to move in, just spend the night there in sleeping bags. We'll claim the land. We stayed there in sleeping bags, and one night led to a couple of weeks. After those two weeks, I knew that it was God's will for us to move.

Julie then came to me and said, "Sonny, I really feel in my heart that God wants us here. The move will be hard on me, but just look at the kids and how much they love being here."

We took our new home of a few months, and gave it to another couple. I told them, "You just take over the payments and it's yours." We both felt strongly that it was God who was giving us this land. We called our beautiful new home "The Hacienda Victoria," which means "Home of Victory."

Chapter Ten

The Hacienda

This was a pivotal time in our ministry. I found myself like clay in the potter's hand. Why had it taken so long and been so difficult for me to understand such a simple truth?

As we were packing boxes, preparing to move to our "House of Victory," I felt I had to share with Julie how the Lord had been impressing on me how much I needed her and how she was a godsend to me; I had realized that she loved the ministry as much as I did and that I had to acknowledge her, not only as my wife, but as my teammate in ministry as well.

I put the box aside and motioned to Julie to come over next to me. A sense of God's love and gratitude overwhelmed me. "Julie, I have to share something with you, bear with me." I swallowed hard, and looked into her eyes. "I know that I haven't always made life easy for you, and I don't think I've ever really let you know how much you mean to me. I want you to know that I love you. I also want you to know that I am realizing more and more everyday how much I need you."

Her eyes welled up with tears. I embraced her and she began to weep in my arms. I think she knew how difficult it was for me to express how much I needed her. She took my hand and said lovingly, "Yes, I know, Sonny. He's shown me the same thing."

She placed her hand on my cheek and said, "Sonny, I love you more than you'll ever know."

With tears streaming down her face, she continued, "I am burying the past hurts and failures in our marriage; I will never again bring them up. Just like the Lord forgave me and has buried my sins, I, too, forgive you. I believe, as I do that, we can become that 'three stranded cord that is not quickly broken,' that God talks about. That's God, you, and me. There is nothing that can stop us. Even if all hell breaks loose against us, together we will be an invincible team!"

We moved to the Hacienda and once again I told Julie that we were going to live like a normal family there. I wasn't planning to take anyone in from the streets. God had done a lot in our marriage by then...the few months that we were alone, we were learning to communicate with one another and I began to spend more and more time with my children. Both of us had learned from our mistakes and our love and commitment to each other was growing.

"Julie," I said, "we'll have meetings here, and maybe baptisms in the pool, and different things like that, but I won't be bringing any men or girls to kick habits here. I think we'll be able to live normal here."

Julie smiled and said, "Oh, Sonny, that sounds so good."

It was a beautiful place, absolutely beautiful. It wasn't built like a house, as it had been a hunting lodge. It was arranged bedroom, rest room, bedroom, rest room, bedroom, rest room, like a motel. You had to walk outside to get to the kitchen, and the big central living room. From our section of the house, it was about a half-block walk.

It was built by Campbell Soup Company. It was quite an old place, with a fireplace in every room. We took three of the rooms, one for Julie and myself, one for our children, and another room for our living room. We needed people to help keep it up because it was so big that two families couldn't do it.

During this time our church was having a new evangelistic thrust. Teams of young girls and guys began going into the streets of Hollywood to witness to the prostitutes. They would leave at midnight and evangelize until three or four in the morning. At first, there wasn't much of a response, but after a few months, the girls were responding and a revival began to take place with the prostitutes.

One night, Julie and I went out to evangelize with

the team. Out of every dingy motel, dark alley, and rat-infested apartment on the side streets swarmed young girls onto the main streets. Teenage girls were standing there half nude. I couldn't help thinking that they were somebody's little girl caught in a web of despair and sin.

The youngest girl we witnessed to that night was nine years old! She got the highest price because many of the customers liked children. We were told the younger the girl, the higher the price. Julie and I walked up to one girl who looked familiar. Sure enough, it was Raindrop. She had lived in our home a few years before. She looked surprised to see us. I could tell she was hurting. She needed a fix.

When she had lived with us, she was a beautiful fourteen-year-old girl and here she was, back on drugs and selling her body. The thing that struck me the most about her was the twitching of her face — it was a constant, uncontrollable nervous twitch that contorted her face.

"Sonny," she said, "I don't need to tell you I need help. Look at me, I'm back on the streets and hooked again." She stretched out her arms to show me her fresh needle marks.

"Come with us," I said. "You don't have to be out here. It's no coincidence that Julie and I ran into you. God has a better life for you." I pleaded with her to ask God back into her life.

As Raindrop listened, her eyes filled with tears..."It's too late for me. I'm too far gone. Sonny, I've never forgotten what I learned when I lived with you and Julie. Those were the best years of my life."

The twitching on her face got worse, affecting her eye and her speech. She stopped for a few seconds until it subsided. She continued, "I wish I could tell you what's in my heart. I can actually feel the presence of evil. I live daily knowing my life is in danger. I'm in constant fear. I wake up at night, alone and scared. I have no one..." she began to cry.

Julie and I could feel her desperation. Suddenly, a car pulled up. An old man yelled out, "Hey Raindrop, how're you doing? Come here." She quickly composed herself, wiping her tears, and fixing her matted hair.

"Bye, Sonny and Julie, I gotta go, that's my customer." I tried to grab her arm and tell her not to go, but she pulled away and ran off.

Julie cried out to her, "Raindrop, don't go...go home with us." She jumped into the car without looking back and sped off.

That night, our hearts were overwhelmed and burdened with the need.

Before we knew it, we had one, two, three rooms, filled with girls. Soon we were again running a huge rehab home. For probably three years there was a revival with those types of girls. None of the rooms locked, so they were able to come into our house if they wanted to. But most of the time they gave us the privacy that we needed.

One time one of the girls overdosed on drugs. One of the guys thought she was sick, but I knew she had been sniffing drugs and had violated the rules of not having drugs on her person or on the property. When I saw her, I yelled, "No, this girl's in an O.D., we've got to get her out of there. Julie, help me put her in the shower. The cold water ought to snap her out of it!"

"Sonny, it's not working," Julie screamed.

"Then let's take her outside and put her in the fish pond," I shouted.

Her body was limp and heavy as several of us went into the water with her. Then we heard a slight moan. "She's coming around. She's coming around. Keep praying!"

We took her out of the water and walked her back and forth all over the place. Finally, after several hours, with God's intervention, she recovered from the O.D. This was a traumatic experience for everyone living there at the Hacienda.

There were times when our children had to move out of their room because we had so many people. I would move them in with us, and the girls who needed to kick their habits would take over their beds. At that time I didn't really think that would affect them, but it did. One time, Julie read in our oldest daughter's diary (she didn't know it was a diary, she thought it was just a little book) where she had written her thoughts about all the people staying in the house. She wrote: "God, I don't like giving up my bed. It's bad enough having to live with all these people. Then there they go again, Mom and Dad are making me give up my bed. I don't like leaving my little place. Why do I have to give up my bed again? I don't like those girls coming and taking over my room."

That shocked us, because we really didn't know that she felt like that. I don't know why, but we didn't realize it. It really made us feel bad, but what could we do? We wanted to help these poor, lost souls so badly that we almost sacrificed our own children.

After reading that, Julie went to Debbie and said, "Sweetheart, we didn't realize how you felt about giving up your bedroom. Jesus has called us to do this work. I know that someday God will do something very special for you. I'm sorry you've had to give up your room, but these girls will die if we don't take them in. I know it's inconvenient for you, but it will be for just a little while." Little did I know that we would continue to use the kids' rooms during the next seven years.

It wasn't all hardships. Some of those years were the happiest years for us, in spite of all the difficulties. We personally had no kitchen, so we had to walk outside, and sometimes in the cold just to get a snack. Soon after we moved to the Hacienda, Julie gave birth to Georgina and a year later, to Timothy.

We set up a little two-burner hot plate in our room and Julie would use it to warm things for them. We had a little refrigerator so we could have something that resembled a kitchen. That part was a little difficult because we didn't have a place to really eat together as a family. We ate most of our meals in the central dining room with the men and women living there.

The Hacienda had such spacious grounds that the children could play outside in safety. We signed them up for organized sports, Bobby Sox, and Little League. This was real healthy for them. I would go every Saturday to their games. I even practiced on the field with them. They all became very good ball players. Our daughter, Debbie, was a state champion. Doreen was a home-run hitter, while Sonny, Jr. developed immensely in the game also. We have over a hundred trophies at home that the kids have won. Because of where we lived, our children didn't get the gang mentality. God really protected them while we lived at the Hacienda.

We had a large swimming pool that everyone was able to enjoy. The children also made good relationships with some of the people we took in. They saw mighty miracles of God almost every day. Many of those people became our closest friends.

One of those girls was Joesy Pineda. She came to us as a young teenager. Two months before I met her, her father had died of alcoholism, leaving a family of nine children. Joesy was the oldest.

As long as she could remember, her father had been a heavy drinker. This caused much turmoil in the home. His health started to rapidly decline and at the age of thirty-five, he was diagnosed with cirrhosis of the liver.

After a fierce fight, her parents separated and Joesy decided to go live with her dad. She and her father had been living together for several months at a cheap motel, when his liver condition flared. She grew worried and thought, What am I going to do if he dies?

She got upset with herself for even thinking that way, but her dad had been in bed for a week and she could see that he was getting worse. Joesy returned to the motel after a long day at school. She noticed that the curtains of their room were closed. Dad always opens the curtains, she thought. When she opened the door, her father was lying there in the dark. She walked closer and noticed that he was barely breathing. "Dad, are you alright?" she asked.

He struggled to talk, and then he responded, "Yeah, I'm alright, Kitten, I'm okay." His body was swollen, like a woman in her ninth month of pregnancy. She knew he was dying. That night, he was rushed to the hospital and in a few days, he was dead.

Joesy's world had fallen apart. She couldn't believe that he was gone. She continued living in that room, hoping and praying that her dad's death was just a nightmare and that some day he would come back.

During this time of grief, someone invited her to church. When I met her, I could see that she was grieving and lonely and that it would take time and a lot of love from the Lord to heal her broken heart, so I invited her to stay with us.

After she had been with us for a few days, I told her, "Come on, let's take a walk." I wanted her to share with me her inner turmoil.

The first few minutes were silent. Then she turned to me and said, "Pastor Sonny, I miss my dad so much, we were so close." She was holding back tears as she continued.

"I know he was a heavy drinker, but he was a good father to us kids. I don't really know if I can ever get over him dying. How could he leave me? I'm only seventeen, I need my dad." We continued walking as she tearfully poured out her heart to me.

"I didn't really know he was an alcoholic. I thought alcoholics were on Skid Row, begging for money. My dad was always home with us, he always worked and supported us. I feel so alone, I feel as if I have no one."

I reached into my pocket and pulled out my Bible. I turned to Psalm 147:3 and began to read, "'He heals the brokenhearted and binds up their wounds.' Joesy, only the Lord can heal your broken heart. He feels your pain and he knows your sorrow."

"He seems so far away, how can He know what I am going through?" she asked.

I responded, "He is a real, living Saviour, and if you ask Him to forgive your sins and come into your heart, He will."

I began to pray for her, as she wept. "Jesus, heal her heart. Forgive her sins, let her know You love her and You are the only one that can heal her broken heart."

After we prayed, the sun broke through the clouds and shone on her tear-stained face. I could see the Lord had begun the work in this brokenhearted teenager.

That night before retiring, I shared Joesy's tragic story with Julie. She felt, as I did, that Joesy needed us and that we were going to not only take this teenager into our "house" but into our "home" and include her into our immediate family.

Our children were blessed as they actually got to experience the power of God during all those years of hardship.

A lot of the girls who came to us off the streets had all sorts of venereal diseases. There were times Julie and I would worry about our children because they would share all the same rest rooms and everything else. When they would come in, we had a policy that they had to be deloused. We then took them to the doctor to make sure they got the proper medication. We would pray the power of the blood of Jesus over them and our kids. We had to believe the Scripture, "I have given you authority to trample on snakes and scorpions and to overcome all the power of the enemy; nothing will harm you"

(Luke 10:19). It's very difficult to describe how terrible they looked and how disease had taken its toll on their once-beautiful bodies. Gradually, we would see the transforming power of God. The Lord would take them and totally change them, so that they looked like virgin saints of God afterwards. They became part of our family. We became very, very close.

Not all the girls found their new life with Christ an easy walk. Some of them were kind of weak. As soon as they got themselves somewhat together they wanted to leave, because many of them had families and some had children who were in different foster homes. Being drug and alcohol free their motherly instincts would return and they desired their children right away. They wanted to establish themselves back into the mainstream of society. Consequently, they would leave too soon and have a fall.

One of the girls, who had been a model and had fallen under Satan's schemes, became a prostitute and drug addict. She had a beautiful conversion experience. Sally had broken free and was gradually growing in the Lord. We felt she would be a real testimony of God's grace and were so happy with all the changes in her life.

We watched the grounds carefully so that the girls' boyfriends, husbands, or pimps would not come in and harm them or take them away against their will.

Sally was a gorgeous, white girl who had a black guy for her pimp. Somehow, one evening this guy pulled up in his decked-out pink Cadillac. He was dressed real flashy, white hat and all. A real hep, cool dude. He looked just like one would imagine a pimp would look like.

We all were surprised that he got onto the grounds. We were all confident that Sally would send him packing, but his influence and hold over her was like that of the devil himself.

When Sally saw him, he motioned for her to get into the car and in spite of our warnings... she was history! In five minutes he possessed her and she was again under the pimp's control and was gone.

We stood there in awe, grief, and silence. We were crushed because none of us thought she would go. She had been totally transformed into a woman of God. That beautiful, beautiful girl was gone. We never saw her again. The hurt and regret went very deep.

Sometimes, Satan would attack us in ways that we never dreamed possible.

Julie:

Even though there were plenty of girls to help me, I still did a lot of the cooking. A few days before Christmas I decided to make cookies. In the midst of all the mess, hands full of oil and flour, one of the guys came into the kitchen saying, "Julie, there are two cops outside and they want to see you. Shall I let them in?"

"Of course. I have no reason not to talk to them. Bring them in," I responded.

I was rather embarrassed when I realized what a mess the kitchen was in. I could tell that the girls helping me were somewhat apprehensive when the two policemen walked into the kitchen.

"Julie Arguinzoni?" one of them asked.

"Yes," I said, "what can I do for you?"

"Your dog was running loose several blocks from your home and we received several complaints. We will have to give you a ticket."

Even though I was taken aback and shocked, I wanted to get back to the baking and said, "Is that all? Officer, would you do me a favor and put the ticket in my apron pocket?"

He did, and they left. That was the last thought I had of the ticket. Early one morning a year later, I heard a loud bang on the door.

I was getting Sonny, Jr., Doreen, and Debbie ready for school. I went to the door and there stood two very big, and I mean big, policemen.

"Are you Julie Arguinzoni?" one asked.

I said, "Yes." I thought they were there for one of the girls or guys.

"We have a warrant for your arrest."

I thought for a moment my legs would give way. "A warrant?" I said. "For what? I've never done anything. I don't even break the traffic laws."

"Oh yes you have." And he started reading "my crime." It was the dog ticket!

Even before he finished I said, "Officer, I'm sorry, you must want my husband. You don't want me. Are you sure it's Julie Arguinzoni? You must want Sonny Arguinzoni, not me."

He answered, "No, it's you we want."

"Let me get my husband," I said.

I ran into the bedroom and Sonny was still asleep. I woke him up, took one look at him, and I started crying. "Oh, Sonny, they're gonna take me to jail!" When I told him why he thought it was the funniest thing he had heard and began to laugh. I didn't think it was funny and started getting upset. After all, it was his dumb dog, not mine! Sonny got up and came with me to talk to the police. They wanted to handcuff me and take me to court. "It's not even mine!" I screamed, "It's not my dog, it's his dog!" as I pointed to Sonny.

My kids were yelling, "Mama, you can't go!" But the police didn't care how many kids I had or anything. I was going to jail.

Sonny finally said, "My name is Pastor Arguinzoni, and this is my wife. Would it be okay with you officers if I take her to court, so you don't have to handcuff her?"

"Okay, Reverend, we'll leave her in your custody then, and you bring her to court at 10 a.m." And they left. I was crying and shaking while Sonny was laughing. He got dressed and took me to court, and there I was, in the middle of all the criminals who had done all kinds of crimes. However, I was there because Sonny's dumb dog had slipped out of the gate.

The judge asked me whose dog it was. I said, "It isn't mine, but I accepted the ticket. Your Honor, it's my husband's dog." He fined me $20 and it was over.

Sonny:

The Hacienda was in a good school district. The school where our children attended had one of the highest academic ratings in the county; but at the same time, there was that pressure...it was such an exclusive area. There was one young boy who came to us for help who was only fifteen years old. We normally didn't take them in that young, but Pepe was an exception.

The first time he ever smoked weed — marijuana — he was eleven years old. By the time he was twelve, he was drinking alcohol, and then became affiliated with a gang.

When he was fourteen, he joined the gang. He could hang out with them, but to become a member, he had to get "jumped" in. What that means is three or four guys beat you up until they think you've had enough. Then they shake your hand, give you a big hug, and say, "You're one of the boys now." Once you're in a gang, you can never really get out.

Pepe was committed to them. They were his security.

One time, some of his friends from the gang went to the house of a rival gang member and knocked on the door. His mother answered the door and said, "My son isn't home." So his friends pushed open the door and hit the woman with a hatchet and killed her. They brutally murdered her and ransacked the house looking for her son. After that, the heat was really on. The police were all over the neighborhood. Victory Outreach evangelism teams were there, too. We had read about this notorious gang in the newspaper and set out to win them to Christ because we had heard of the hatchet murder and the gangs.

Once in the gang, Pepe's goals were to go to San Quentin Prison, join the Mexican Mafia, and have his body covered with tattoos. He also wanted to have the biggest moustache, because that was a symbol of machoism. He wanted the biggest moustache that ever went into San Quentin yard. He thought he was either going to be a drug addict, or in prison for the rest of his life.

Pepe got caught stealing a car and was taken to jail. His wish was coming true. At his court appearance, instead of sending him to jail, the judge allowed him to go to our rehab home in Victorville. He wasn't there a month, before he accepted Jesus as his Saviour. He then wanted "Jesus Christ" tattooed on his arm.

We then brought him to the Hacienda to live with us. Julie and I became his legal guardians. We grew to love him as our very own.

Julie talked with him when he moved in. "Look, Pepe," she said, "you gotta be good because of all the young boys who will come behind you. We want to help them too, and you're the first one, so we want you to do good and set an example."

Pepe was a special kid. He had suffered a lot as a young boy and I felt he needed us at this point in his life. "Pepe," I said, "you just stay close to God and you'll see — He will use you greatly one day. Not only that, but remember you will be going to school with my children, so remember this...don't embarrass them."

At school he started a Bible study that met every day, Monday through Friday. He met at lunchtime with about four or five kids. He even had a rally on campus with about sixty young people showing up. He preached all about the free gift of God, which is eternal life.

What a delight Pepe was to us as a family. We could see the hand of God on his life. His graduation from high school was a joy for all of us. He received the Rotary Club Citizenship award.

He was given a standing ovation from the students and teachers alike. Julie and I stood there, as did our children, and many people from the church, crying like babies. Our special boy had made it. God gave us in Pepe a very special Treasure Out of Darkness.

Chapter Eleven

Under Surveillance

Our church on St. Louis Street was about twenty-five minutes of freeway driving from the Hacienda. We filled my car up, packed the "Jesus Van" up and all went to church.

The Lord was increasing our congregation and the ministry was growing by leaps and bounds. We were then all challenged with another step of faith. We had been renting the Hacienda when we got a call that the owner wanted to sell the place to us.

"Pastor Sonny," he said, "I'll sell this property to you for $125,000. You can buy it with $25,000 down. I know it's worth a lot more but I believe in what you folks are doing."

We all knew that he could have gotten twice that much, so we decided in faith that we would buy the property. In a miraculous way we raised the down payment within the church, and were able to secure the property. We could see the Spirit of God moving in a mighty way.

As I said before, this was a very exclusive, high-income area. There were people who would call up city hall, complaining that we were running a drug center with dope everywhere. I had to go to city hall a number of times and talk with them. We suspected that the police were wire-tapping our phones. The undercover surveillance began after I had met this man who was a very well-known gangster. He had been a high-ranking member of the Mafia, but I overlooked the stigma that my association with him might bring because I felt he was really hungry for God. I started inviting him over to the Hacienda, so I could share Christ with him.

One day he came in his stretched limo, and all his cronies with him. I knew it was dangerous, because I had heard that the mafia had a contract out on him. Since he was so hungry for God, I figured it was worth the chance trying to win him to the Lord. I spent much time with him, talking to him about Jesus. Because of that, I believe the police started a surveillance on us. I would pick up the phone, not only would I hear the clicks of the recorder, but sometimes the wires would cross and you could hear the police talking to each other. We knew that we were even being followed.

One night we came home and found squad cars and police all over the place. I couldn't believe my eyes but we were being raided. Now what are the neighbors going to think, I thought.

Without notice they descended on us like locusts. They broke down doors and ransacked where the guys were sleeping. They thoroughly searched the entire complex inside and out, looking for drugs. Everyone on the grounds were terrified that this could be done. Especially because they were now clean.

I asked them, "Officers, what are you doing? What are you looking for?"

"We're looking for someone," one replied.

In drawers? I thought to myself. They left without fixing the doors, or repairing the damage. They never apologized or anything. They thought for sure that they were gonna find some drugs or something, but they never did.

That was a miracle of God for there were instances when these guys, before they were saved, did sneak drugs in and we didn't know it.

We had some incidents where we could tell that they did, because they would be nodding out under the influence of drugs.

One day this guy came in with $10,000 worth of drugs that he had on consignment. He had got the stuff, and was supposed to sell it, keep some money for himself, then turn in the rest. He came over just to visit. I talked to him about Jesus and he gave his life to the Lord. He had an instant deliverance and I could see the change in his eyes. God cleansed him. The following day he came and showed us this bag of drugs. We looked into the bag and it was heroin.

"Here, Sister Julie, take this and flush it down the toilet," he said, as he handed her the bag.

"Are you sure you want to do this? Why don't you take it back to the guy you got it from?" I asked. I knew what he was doing was real dangerous, as he had to pay for this stuff.

"Sonny, Jesus has really convicted me now that I'm a Christian (about twelve hours old). If I return this stuff it's going to fall into the hands of someone else who is going to use it. I know that God wants me to give it to you guys so you can destroy it. Whatever happens, me and Jesus are going to face it together."

Julie took the bag and headed for the bathroom, and we were right behind her. We were headed for a celebration. Julie opened up the bag and began pouring it down the toilet. We were all shouting, "Praise the Lord," and "Thank You, Jesus." It was so beautiful and powerful seeing the Spirit of God at work in our midst. He did protect this fellow and he continued serving the Lord.

Our suspicions of being under surveillance were proven a year later, when one of the police officers who was a Christian, told us. Officer Bob, had been telling the police department, "These people are straight and trying to do a good work. You are not going to find anything on these people." They didn't believe him.

After the year of surveillance was over, he came and told me, "I know you probably thought that you were going crazy with the wire-tapping and all that. I want you to know that it was true. You were under surveillance for a year. They found you were clean, clean, clean. It was beautiful for me to be able to remind the department that all along I had been telling them that they were not going to find anything on you. And they didn't."

Julie:

A few weeks after Joesy came to our home, she began smiling again. Before long, our kids were calling her their big sister. She joined our office staff and in a short time, became Sonny's secretary. The Lord had brought this beautiful, young girl into our lives and into our family.

A year later, a young man who had given his life to Christ and graduated from our rehabilitation home came to work in our office as a court liaison. His name was Steve. He had grown up in Santa Paula, California. By the time he was twenty-four years old, he had been using heroin for seven years. During that time he had been arrested thirty-three times.

Joesy and Steve worked in the same office and soon became friends, fell in love, and two years later, they were married.

They both expressed to Sonny and me a deep desire for full-time ministry. They had caught the vision of taking a city for God. We could see that they would some day be used greatly for Him. They got involved in different areas of the church, gaining knowledge in order to produce a fruitful ministry.

Although Steve was unpolished in many of his ways, he had a teachable spirit and a profound love for God. His eagerness to share the gospel in the streets and jails was infectious to others. Throughout this time, they were continuously being molded and discipled for future ministry.

Sonny:

It was a joy for us when Steve and Joesy invited us to their cozy apartment one evening after church at the Montebello High School. I know that the Lord had been dealing with them about going out and establishing a work. They had been faithful in their areas of ministry in the church for several years.

Steve began to anxiously share, "Pastor Sonny, last week, I went to visit Gilbert and Diane in San Francisco. Their church is doing great!"

His eyes glistened with excitement as he spoke. "They've only been there a short time and their church is growing. Ed and Mitzi are doing good, too! I feel the Lord wants Joesy and I to go to Hayward, California. I've canvassed the area. I've seen the need there and..." his eyes welled up with tears. He couldn't continue. A beautiful presence filled the room. Steve began to cry.

"Joesy, how do you feel," I asked.

"Steve and I have been praying and I know it will be very difficult for me to leave my church and you and Julie and the kids, but the Lord has reassured me that He would give me many spiritual children if I'm obedient to his call."

Julie and I were blessed to hear what was on their hearts. We knew that these young people we had learned to love dearly, had found their city. We sensed the presence of the Holy Spirit and joined hands and prayed, thanking God for His leading.

Once again Julie started desiring to have a place for the family. We had been living at the Hacienda for about seven years. "Julie, why don't you start making out plans of what you want, and I'll build you a house on this property," I told her.

Julie said, "Oh sure, you're gonna build me a house, you don't have any money to build me a house."

"Just draw up the plans that you want, and we will build it here on the grounds," I responded.

She said, "Okay." She even got an architect, and they started drawing out all the plans that she wanted. She drew them exactly the way she felt we needed for our size family. She had some definite ideas; she wanted it to be a two-story house with two sinks in the master bathroom; the whole family had always shared one sink.

"While I'm at it, why don't I ask the Lord to give me two fireplaces, one in the family room and one in our bedroom. I want a step-up, raised bathtub in the master bath."

She was having a real fantasy drawing up those plans. She wanted a sunken living room and windows — a lot of them — but the bedroom window must face the east so the morning sun would shine through.

When the plans were all drawn out and finished, I said, "Now put them up on the wall where you can see them every day and just start praying for them. I'm going to build it right here on the property."

Julie started praying for that house everyday for a year.

She was real happy that the house would be built on the Hacienda property because our children were already established in school, and that was one of the few stabilities they had.

Julie printed the Scripture, "My father owns the cattle on a thousand hills" and "My God shall supply all your needs according to His riches and glory," and put them on the refrigerator. She prayed, "My God, my God, You can do anything. You own everything."

Down the street, about a block and a half away, there were some two-story houses being built. "Sonny, why don't we go by there and see them?" Julie asked.

"Yeah, let's go see them," I said.

We took another couple from the church with us. As we walked into one of those houses Julie said, "I feel something peaceful here!"

The other fellow said, "I feel the peace, too!"

We all seemed to feel something. "This must be where the sunken living room is going to be," Julie said. It wasn't carpeted or anything as yet. We looked around a little bit more and left. We went back again a few weeks later when they had finished more of the house. As we walked into the different rooms, Julie started noticing all the things that she had asked God for on those plans. "They're all here. There's two sinks over here, there's a fireplace in the family room and in the bedroom. The bath in the master bedroom is raised. The sun was shining brightly from the east into the master bedroom." We went into the sunken living room. We all joined hands and prayed, "Lord, if this is Your will for us to have this house, then You make it happen, because we don't have any money.

As we were in the circle, praying, we all felt the presence of God. It was so beautiful the way the Lord made us feel that it was going to be our house.

Without Julie knowing it, I made all the arrangements and bought the house. It took me about three weeks. It was only done with God's help, blind faith, and "guts."

When the salesman handed me the key, I couldn't wait to get home and give it to Julie. For fourteen years she had been sharing our house or living in a rehab home situation.

When I arrived back at the Hacienda, Julie and the

kids were out playing on the lawn.

"Julie, bring the kids and come here for a moment. I have something for you. Meet me halfway!" I shouted.

"What do you have?" she asked.

"You'll see, you'll see!" I teased.

Slowly, I took my hands from behind my back and dangled the key in front of them.

"What's that for?" Debbie asked.

"Yeah, Dad, what's that key for?" chimed in Georgina.

Julie's eyes got bigger and bigger as they filled with tears. "Sonny is it? No, it couldn't be. Sonny, what's that key to. Sonny, is it? Please say something!" Julie exclaimed.

"Here, Honey, this is the key to your new home."

She and the kids started yelling and jumping all over the place.

"Man, you really did it! You really got it!" Julie shouted.

"Yeah, it's your very own key. Come on, let's go and open the house," I said.

We got all the kids together and said, "Come on, let's go see our new home." When Julie opened the door, and saw it was all finished, she yelled, "Oh, thank you, Jesus. I have my own dishwasher, my own stove, my own refrigerator, even my own trash compactor. I have too many things at one time. Sonny, it is almost too much for me. I think I am going to have a heart attack. I'm getting sick, it's just too much for me."

Of course, we didn't have any furniture, curtains, drapes, etc. The kids started running upstairs, "This is my bedroom, oh, this is my bedroom." I mean it looked so big to them because they had never had their own rooms. They were always all in one room. Julie and I and our five children, living in two rooms, and then all of a sudden we had all this room. It was just absolutely too much. However, that's exactly the kind of Heavenly Father who loves us. He has even promised to give us the desires of our hearts. There is nothing that we give up in this life that God hasn't promised to bless us with a hundredfold.

Chapter Twelve

Saying "No" to the Government

The vision of "East L.A. for Jesus," burned within me. Until this point, we had planted only one church in Pico Rivera and people were beginning to take notice of the miracles that were happening in our little church.

A group of people in Monterey Park, California had heard about our outreach to troubled youth and gave us a church building. They were a church that had decided to disband and their board chose to give the property to Victory Outreach free and clear; they wanted us to reach their community for Christ. It was a beautiful little church. We sent a small team to have services there, and in a short time it was filled with young people.

We continued to aggressively go to the streets and the alleyways to preach. We found a place in the heart of the city that was infested with junkies. The area was called Maravilla, which means, "The Miracle." Years earlier, we had won our first convert there...his name was Bobby. He then led his mother and brother, Cal, to the Lord.

Cal was also a hard-core junkie. After his conversion, he grew in the Lord and turned out to be a tremendous preacher. Cal was one of the most notorious men in the area. He was a "boss" while in prison and had a reputation of respect and honor. Cal was a guy you did not mess with. He was loyal to the gangs and as a result was very loyal to the ministry and to me, when he became a Christian. As soon as he was saved he wanted to do something, and he started teaching the children in Sunday School. He was willing to do whatever it was that had to be done. I could see God's hand on him, so I sent him to Bible school; he was eager to learn. He became one of my assistants and had a real desire for the ministry.

Cal had so much drive I soon noticed that his vision went beyond East L.A. He started praying for San Bernardino, and sharing with me how the Lord was dealing with him about going there. San Bernardino is about an hour's drive from Los Angeles. I was just trying to reach our Jerusalem, East L.A., but now the Lord was taking us beyond and raising up a young man who was going to expand that vision.

I recognized that if I would keep him, even though I

felt we needed him in the church, I would eventually lose him. He would lose that fire and the vision that he had inside of him. When we announced to the church that Cal was going to be sent out to San Bernardino, some of the guys asked me, "Pastor Sonny, why do we have to let Cal go? We don't want him to go." Some of the families in the church were very attached to him.

"Because we must be faithful and obey the Great Commission," I said. It was beautiful that we felt such a love between us. I also had a hard time releasing Cal because he gave the guys within the church and rehab home such a good example in loyalty. He was what you call in the streets a "back to back partner." In the beginning, every time I released a pastor to go to another city, I had to struggle with the church to let them go.

We sent out Cal and his wife, Beatrice, out into San Bernardino.

We gave him eight people so he could form a team. He had gotten a house where he and the team would live. The team consisted of men and women who were ex-drug addicts and gang members who could help him in reaching out to the people in the neighborhood. He began a rehabilitation home in his house.

We sent him other teams (on a daily basis) to start evangelizing the streets. We knew he needed financial help, so we helped him with his rent and food, until he could get himself established. We figured we would help him financially for a year. It was a very low budget because we didn't have much money ourselves.

He became successful and soon he had a home full of men and women. He then found a building and started having church services, and the work began to grow.

The church on St. Louis was growing numerically, as well, and the outreach programs were expanding. We were on our way, with God's help.

"Arline and Mando were testifying in the prison yesterday," Joe exclaimed. "Man, are they anointed. Mando played the guitar and sang a duet with Arline; about seventy-five hard-core prisoners went to the altar and gave their lives to Christ. The Lord is really using them, Pastor Sonny."

Reports about this precious couple sharing the gospel under the anointing were steadily coming to my ears. Everywhere they went: prisons, streets, and churches, people gave their lives to Christ.

I rejoiced as I remembered from where they had come. Mando, an ex-con, and Arline, delivered from childhood hurts and resentments. Now the Lord was using their past failures for good. As they would speak, hurting people could identify with them. We were also receiving reports about Pepe.

Pepe was beginning to hold youth revivals and we were also using him in our church to develop our youth ministry. He was maturing rapidly. Everywhere he went, young people were giving their lives to Christ.

The Lord had blessed him with a powerful preaching ministry.

Along with pastors being raised up to take cities...evangelists were also playing a vital role in the training and edifying of the churches.

Meanwhile, Saul the Vietnam vet, who several years before had come in on Gless Street, with his long hair in a ponytail, had shown a real desire for ministry. I could see that people held him in a position of respect and they were drawn to him for advice. By now, he was a Bible school graduate and was studying for his B.A. degree at Southern California College. Along with his growth of Bible knowledge, he had matured in his character and personality.

I began to see the Lord unfolding His plan, and as my workload multiplied, I knew I needed someone on my staff that I could lock arms with; someone who had captured my vision to establish our mother church as a strong base without a desire to plant his own church. I needed someone I could trust. All along, the Lord had been preparing Saul for this ministry.

One day, he shared with me, "Pastor Sonny, I was birthed here and I've been under your leadership for several years. I have walked with you and watched you closely, and I believe in what we're doing as a ministry. I want to assist you and help you build disciples. I know the workload is heavy. There is much you want to see accomplished for God, and just like Aaron and Hur held up the arms of Moses, I want to hold up your arms!'

I could see the sincerity in his eyes as he chose his words carefully. He continued, "I want you to know my wife and I have prayed about this for some time and we're eager and ready to be of service to you and Julie. Pastor Sonny, I'm willing to give my life, if need be, for the sake of the gospel."

Knowing he was not a man who used flowery words, I was deeply moved. The Lord brought Saul into my life to stand by my side through thick and thin; and to be my Timothy in the faith. By his commitment and love for Christ and me, he would teach others, by his example, how to be a true soldier of Jesus Christ. The government, during this period, was giving out money for programs such as ours, and there were many people who were getting what they called "a piece of the pie." They told us that we could be getting money from the government, especially for the type of work that we were doing. I looked at the workers and felt sorry for them, because I knew that many of them were sacrificing to their limits. Suddenly there would be money available so that they would be able to receive salaries. We put a proposal together for one year to see how it would work.

We were funded to the tune of $150,000. With that funding we were able to pay salaries to the workers. Gradually, I began to notice that there was a change that began to take place within the workers and in the ministry. Before, when we reached the drug addicts and gang members, we would bring them in, lay hands on them, and pray for them. Now as they came in, there were applications that needed to be filled out because of the documentation that the government required. The mentality began to change. Instead of looking at them as souls needing Christ, we began to adopt the mentality and language of the federal programs, referring to them as clients instead of souls. That's when I felt that we were headed for a real problem and possible downfall.

"Dear God," I said, "our ministry is becoming more like a social program than a ministry." Thank God the contract that we had with the government was for only one year. After I made up my mind this wasn't God's will for us, they called and told us that they were willing to fund us again, and even give us double. They were offering to give us $300,000. Believe me, that was very tempting. Especially when we didn't have any money. I had a meeting with the staff, and shared with them how I felt that if we kept on going with the government that we were going to be losing out in the long run. We would lose the anointing, and it was the anointing that had given us the success. If we put our trust in God, then He would be able to meet our needs.

"There must never be compromise in our ministry," I said.

"The other day when one of the girls answered the

phone and said, 'God Bless You,' the person calling strongly suggested, 'You shouldn't say God Bless You, that's not professional. We read in Hebrews 9:22 that without shedding of blood there is no remission [of sin].'

"Jesus Christ shed His blood on Calvary for us, and said, said in John 14:6, 'I am the way, the truth, and the life: no man cometh unto the Father, but by me.'

"That is our message! That is our purpose! That is our hope! There is absolutely no other position we must ever take. The Word of God is absolute. Jesus Christ is all or He is nothing at all! The government can never be our source.

"I feel that we must go back to working by faith. We will have to be willing to rough it, and sacrifice. Even though we will be sacrificing, we can be assured that the blessing of God will be upon our lives and the ministry," I said.

They all agreed unanimously, as they began to take inventory of the past year. The best way to go was totally by faith. We turned down the offer, and as soon as we did many people started hearing about it. They couldn't believe we turned down $300,000. People, even politicians, commended us for our convictions, and for the stand that we had taken.

During this time of readjustment, we realized how we had gotten sidetracked. The Lord had led me years before to start a "church" and that out of the "local church" would flow all the other ministries needed to help build the kingdom of God. The year that we received federal funding, all of our efforts were diverted into building the rehabilitation program. We had to come back to our foundational concepts of building a strong church base combined with sacrificial giving and the discipling and developing of men and women. They then would take the gospel to the four corners of the earth.

As we continued to put the emphasis on the church we were able to expand to other cities, such as Pomona, Compton, and Long Beach. These were established by our own men who were trained, discipled, and educated within the ministry. God not only expanded, but began multiplying our vision. Most of these men, after establishing their work began to also plant churches.

We were invading Satan's territory and I knew that he was mad. We were in an all-out war!

Our ministry is certainly involved in discipleship — but Satan wants us telling people where to live, whom to date, what to eat, etc., when God wants us to train them in the Word, how to hear His voice and serve Him only!

In the past, the Church has been off-balance about inner-healing, demons, shepherding, discipleship, faith, prosperity, miracles, etc. All of the above are truth, but when out of balance, they can become a stumbling block to believers.

One of our men who began to expand his ministry,

who had a lot of men under him, got caught up in an unbalanced view of discipleship through another ministry. With some of these men there is always the danger that with all of their zeal they can become sidetracked and out of balance.

For years we in the Church have gone from one new thing to the next. Satan doesn't care what we do as long as he can get us lopsided, and then the truth becomes ineffective.

This is what happened with one of our young pastors that we had groomed for ministry. He started getting out of balance and following another minister who had exclusive ways of discipleship. What I mean by exclusive discipleship is that they would tell him everything that he had to do, causing him not to think for himself. Also, they were anti-everybody else, and had an cliquish spirit. They thought they were the only ones who were right, and making an impact in the world.

This fellow got so caught up and so impressed with their ministry, that he started going to their conferences, and started taking men with him. I began to notice that he was not only taking a different route, with a different philosophy of ministry, but he was also influencing men from his church. When we had our conferences, he and his disciples were preaching to our men their "new" discipleship doctrine.

As a result, there was a division that began to develop. I tried to talk to him a number of times, but I could see that he was getting direction elsewhere.

I could tell that this young man wasn't a part of us anymore. He was totally being led by someone else and following another ministry that I knew would eventually have serious problems, because of its methods of "discipleship on demand."

Several pastors tried to talk to him about his new ideas on discipleship and his desire to follow another group. One man actually challenged him by saying, "You mean to tell us that you're not going to listen to your pastor? Your pastor's telling you to stay here for six months and get plugged in to what God is doing here."

He replied, "No, I can't, because I get my direction from over there."

At that point, I felt I needed to release him. I told him, "If you can't disengage yourself for six months, then you go with them. If any of the pastors you sent out from your church want to go with you, take them."

They changed their name and that was the first time we experienced a split within our ranks.

I've always had the conviction that we must be discipling people, not to ourselves, but to the Lord. The building of disciples must be totally for God's glory alone. We have tried to maintain a covenant relationship with the pastors who have been sent out. This type of structure allows for accountability, encouragement, and the ability to reach out to each other while enduring the struggles of ministry. I've realized that the parent/child relationships that our churches have with each other come from the bond of love and not manipulation.

I knew we were reaching our limits at the St. Louis Street church. Our attendance was now running around 500. In our struggle to establish strong committed people, we noticed a common thread among them. Many were holding on to "things" within their lives that hindered their commitment to the Lord.

We knew that unless they discarded these stumbling blocks, they would have a link to their past life that could eventually draw them back.

We read in Acts 19:19 where believers who had confessed Jesus as Lord, had gathered all their former teachings and burned them publicly. Through that Scripture, we developed what we called "The Old Man Barrel."

We would ask people to bring to church any article that they felt was hindering them or causing them to stumble from their commitment to the Lord.

We had numerous items brought that surprised us all. Most of the items no one knew about, since it was personal. After addressing the Scripture, "...old things are passed away, behold all things become new," I would ask them to come forward. As they came, they brought hundreds of "oldie but goodie" albums, drugs, pills, cigarettes, etc.

Each person would go up to the "Old Man Barrel" and share with the congregation how these articles had hindered their life for the last time. As they threw them in the barrel, there was a release that was felt throughout the room. There were some items that were brought which seemed hard to understand how they could be a stumbling block to their Christian walk. One in particular was a Karate outfit. When the young man brought it in and stood before the congregation, I looked at him in disbelief. I said, "You don't have to put this in the barrel. It's okay for you to keep."

He looked at me with genuine openness and said, "Pastor Sonny, for someone else, it might not be a stumbling block, but for me it is."

When he threw his outfit and shoes in the barrel, I could see people re-evaluating their commitments as well.

The church was not only growing, but the people were growing in the Lord, and they began to fully understand the principles of tithing. They were sacrificing for the work of the kingdom. God, of course, had also shown me the principle of tithing and giving. Julie was right all along. I was simply slow in the area of finances. Praise God that my people learned that principle more quickly than I did.

Chapter Thirteen

The Vision Expands

I read the letter over and over. Was it really true what I was reading? Julie and I were invited to come to England to minister. An organization had heard of us and wanted us to speak at rallies and crusades all over England.

"Julie, you will never believe what we are going to do!" I shouted as I came in the door. "We are going to England."

"We are going where? When? Sonny, why are we going to England? We can't afford to do anything like that! Sonny, what do you mean?" Julie quizzed.

"Honey, it won't cost us a cent. This organization wants us to come and is paying all of our expenses. It's true we are going across the ocean. Can you believe that?"

Julie and I were like two kids on their first day of school. The flight to London was awesome. We could hardly believe that God would allow us to do such a thing. From the ghetto of East Los Angeles to a fancy hotel in Picadilly Circus.

We were amazed at all the cars driving on the wrong side of the street. Even though we hadn't held a meeting yet, I took Julie's hand and said, "Can you imagine, Julie... look where God has brought us."

For the first time God had us with a different kind of people that spoke with a different accent, and had a different culture. We were even wondering if our ministry would really come across, and be effective, so far away from home.

Our time in England was very special to us. It was one of the very few times in our married life that we had been alone, where we could share, talk, and just get to know each other. It was a very spiritual time of thinking, praying, and preparing ourselves for what God had in store.

As the rallies began, especially the first one, we were absolutely amazed at the size of the building. It held hundreds, and we wondered if anyone would come. To our amazement there was standing room only. As we looked at the audience Julie turned to me and said, "Sonny, they all look so sophisticated and educated. Do you think they will accept what we have to say?"

"Honey," I responded, "I've been thinking the same thing. God is here, and we'll just follow the leading of the Lord and do what He says. The results will be His."

We decided that Julie would share first. I could tell she was a little nervous, but she got up there and the anointing of God fell on her. She started sharing our simple stories of what God was doing in East Los Angeles. I could tell, just by the move of the Spirit, that the young people were responding, and they held on to every word that she spoke.

Then I was given the opportunity to speak. I simply preached the Word and included my testimony of how God had absolutely freed me of heroin overnight. I could sense that these people genuinely loved us in the Lord and were responding excitedly to what we were saying. When I gave the altar call the young people started streaming forward. They wanted to hear more about God's deliverance. Oh, how moving it was to see these British young people weeping, accepting Jesus as their Saviour, and then desiring deliverance from all sorts of sin.

When the meeting was over very few left. They wanted to talk, and to share, and just show their appreciation to us. Julie and I were awed at the wonderful way God had used us. Every city we went to was the same. The halls and centers were packed out. We were invited to be guests in various homes during our stay. That was a special delight to get to know these people, and they us, and to be able to share mutual visions of reaching the inner cities for Christ.

Here are some excerpts from a letter written by Julie

a few days after we arrived:

Dear Mom and Dad,

Greetings from England! The need here is great...every minute is filled with excitement and new adventure. It's hard to believe how although we're thousands of miles away, the needs are the same. A fifteen-year-old girl came up to me tonight, she was a junkie and wanted help. She had come to the rally and heard Sonny speak, but she couldn't believe he had been a junkie; until he rolled up his sleeve and she saw his inner arm with his old line of scars. This gathered a crowd of junkies around us...England is full of teenagers, plagued with this horrendous habit, Mom. Sonny and I wish we could take them all home. I miss the kids so much, but I need to be with my husband. I feel that every so often, a couple should go off alone; back away from the ministry and find each other. Also, as you back away, you get a good perspective on what you are endeavoring to do for the Lord.

I love you,
Julie

It was great for Julie and me not to be under the pressure of the ministry at home. I was able to think more clearly, and God began showing me that we needed to take another step of faith. Not only of stepping out of our building on St. Louis Street, but enlarging our vision more and more. There was a world out there going to hell, and God wanted us to tell them about His saving grace, His deliverance, and the pure joy and excitement of knowing Him. God encouraged us day after day. He strengthened our faith. He shook us to the very foundation of our beings so that we could go back with a new vision and new determination to advance for His Kingdom. Going to England was a confirmation that God had greater things for us to do. He put in our hearts a much wider purpose for us in the establishing of our ministry; to become a sending church, thrusting laborers into the harvest fields that were white, ready for harvest.

When Julie and I returned to East Los Angeles we were excited and inspired at what God was going to do. I gave myself to the church with renewed vigor. Julie said, "Sweetheart, I am going to give it all I have, too." With our five children, Debbie, Doreen, Sonny, Jr., Georgina, and Timothy, Julie had a lot of responsibilities at home, and now this renewed thrust also added more work to her already busy day.

After that first visit to England, we were invited often by the brethren there. On two occasions we took our choir and toured the country having meetings in the open air, in auditoriums and in churches. I remember on one of the tours we took, Rudy, Joesy, Steve, Pepe, Philip, Saul, and Stella, and about forty others. When our young men and women testified, it was phenomenal.

During one of the meetings, I called Pepe up to give

his testimony. He shared how the Lord had delivered him from a life destined for hell. He got really excited and began challenging the youth. Under the anointing of God's Holy Spirit, he proclaimed, "Jesus is alive. He is my Lord and my Deliverer. I challenge you young people to accept Jesus as your Lord. He will come into your heart."

The auditorium was silent; you could hear a pin drop, except for Pepe compelling them, with boldness and authority. "We've come over five thousand miles to tell you that Jesus died for your sins. He wants to forgive you. He's here right now waiting to come into your life."

Words were just flowing from Pepe to these hungry youth. "The Word of God says that if thou confess with thy mouth, the Lord Jesus and believe in thine heart, He that God has raised from the dead, thou shall be saved. Therefore, he who the son sets free is free indeed."

Julie and I were so blessed to see the Lord using Pepe.

When we left England, God had placed a burning desire in our hearts to return and establish a work there.

The Montebello High School opened up to us and we all felt that it was God's will for us to go into this school auditorium. We rented it and began holding services there. The auditorium seated 1,800 people, so when we first moved in there with our 500, it seemed as though we had no congregation at all. Very soon, the congregation began to grow from 500 to 600, then to 700. We knew then that we had made the right choice. The ministry had expanded to various cities and the outreach was increasing almost daily. We decided that we ought to have a conference and bring all of our men and the various members together and have a time of sharing, worship, and ministry. We held our first conference on St. Louis Street.

Our second conference was held at the high school. We had so much in common with the pastors coming in from the various cities. We could identify with the hard times of the ministry, and the Spirit of the Lord gave us the ability to even laugh at some of these hardships. The women would get together and exchange views about their husbands and the way God was moving in their lives. We had a glorious time together. You could feel the bond of love that we had for one another. This is probably one of the most beautiful and precious things about our ministry. We not only grew numerically, but in love for one another. When we came together and saw each other it was such a time of joy and refreshment. What seemed strange to me was that they began calling me their spiritual father, and Julie their spiritual mother. In a way that was really true, because we loved these people almost as much as we loved our own children.

As they came for the meetings we chuckled as we saw them, because many of them looked as though they had been dragged off the battlefield. Most of them were barely making it financially, and you could see the strain and stress of battle fatigue on their faces. It was such a serious time for them feeding on the Word, and establishing relationships, but we also had the joy of hearing all the war stories that everyone had to share. Those stories served to show how God had been faithful in the midst of the combat.

At the Wednesday morning gathering we had three preaching services. At the end of the last service, I told everyone they were dismissed, except those who wanted to stay behind and pray. Ed was there with a friend from the church who wanted to go to the altar to pray, so he just sat in the pew and waited for him.

Ed Morales is a large man with the typical very heavy, black mustache. He is tattooed and dark-complexioned. When he came to the rehab home, he was tough and hard. As Ed sat in the pews praying, the Holy Spirit moved on him in a very unique and powerful way. Ed came to me weeping, looking like "Gentle Ben" after the service and told me, "Pastor Sonny, I was sitting there in the pew and I heard a voice that said, 'I am the Lord, who has called you and chosen you...' I broke down crying."

I looked at Ed as he stood there, and I laid my hands on him and prayed. When I laid my hands on him and prayed, he just fell apart crying again. He cried for three days. A few months later on July 1, Ed and Mitzi arrived in San Jose, California.

Chapter Fourteen

The NIGHTCLUB

One of the unique things we did at the high school was to put on plays and invite the community and gang members to come. That also proved to be a blessing of God. The auditorium would be packed every time we did this, and there would be many decisions for Christ that would follow. That also led us a step further in that we had all of these converts who now needed follow-up and teaching, and establishment into the faith. That necessitated us starting a firm system of follow-up in teaching.

About the same time, Trinity Broadcasting Network gave us a half hour time slot on their television network. I appointed Julie as my producer, and we began producing our own television program which was called "Treasures Out of Darkness." Of course we got this title from the verse that Dick Mills had given me years before. The television show presented our work to a very vast audience, and soon we had many different people starting to attend our church, because it was announced that our services were held at the Montebello High School auditorium.

That took some real adjusting for Julie and I. Basically, until that time I had been working with drug addicts and gang members, and those coming in off of the streets. Now I had to learn to work with transfer growth — people that would come from other churches that were already Christians, but with different backgrounds.

Two young brothers by the names of Raul and David had come to us hooked on drugs. After a year in our rehabilitation home under the discipleship of Rudy, they came to me and expressed a desire to be in full-time ministry.

I sent them to the streets to evangelize, and before long, I began to see them develop. I then put them to work in our home Bible study groups and drew them closer, training them in a model apprenticeship.

During this time, David developed a relationship with a beautiful, young girl named Donna. She had been a gang member before coming to Christ and was active in our gang outreach, discipling other girls.

After a brief courtship, David and Donna were married. They asked Raul to live with them. These young people were eager to be used of God.

I can remember many times meeting with them and their disciples, some of them just teenagers. We would stay talking for hours on end about the ministry. I took time with them because I could see that the Lord had a special work for them to do.

Here was a group of young ex-dopers and street-wise kids, seemingly insignificant, but with such a burning compassion for the lost.

One evening after church, I invited them over to my house. They all gathered around, anxious for a word of encouragement.

"Pastor Sonny," Raul asked, "you preach about the vision all the time. I'm beginning to understand it, but for the benefit of these young guys, could you share your heart with us?"

They listened attentively. "The Word of God says in Proverbs 29:18, 'Where there is no vision, the people perish.' That's why I believe in instilling vision into young people, so that they can see what I see."

"What do you see, Pastor Sonny?" Donna asked.

"I see hundreds of cities that need the gospel. All over the world, there is a need for young people like yourself to go and do the very same thing we are doing right here in Los Angeles. They need the same revival we're experiencing. You have seen how God is using Ed and Mitzi in San Jose, and how the Lord is using Cal to establish a church in San Bernardino. Look at Philip and Pepe, who are now evangelists. He can also use you to do the very same thing."

They all looked at each other. There was a hush in the room as they listened, motionless. Augie broke the

207

silence and said, "I believe it...we may be young and I know we're not prepared, but we can identify with young people in any city."

"That's right, Augie. You can go to any city in the world and the needs of young people are the same. Drugs, sex, and all kinds of sin is rampant everywhere. The language may be different, and the culture may not be the same, but their need for a redeeming Saviour to break the bondage of sin are the same. People are crying for an answer. 'The fields are ready, they are white.' I believe some of you will be called to go."

I knew that several of them felt the call of God to go into the work of the Lord full time. I could especially see the hand of God on little Augie and the two brothers, Raul and David.

"Pastor Sonny, what are the first steps in breaking a city open?" David asked with anticipation.

"You must first have a vision for that city, a vision that consumes you. You can't be effective if it's only your pastor's vision. You must have it burned into your own heart by God. A vision is caught, not taught. Also, you must know that you play a vital role in the destiny of this ministry, no matter how insignificant you may feel.

"Take for example the apostles. Jesus gave them a worldwide task to fulfill in Matthew 18:18-20. Even though they may have felt like nobodies, they were totally saturated with a sense of their mission. They knew that God had chosen them as He is choosing you this very hour."

"Wow! That's heavy stuff," said 16-year-old Tony. "But you could have big dreams and vision and it won't do you any good unless you tell someone."

"That's right," I said. "Lots of people dream, but to be effective, we must evangelize and share the gospel. We must tell them there's power in the name of Jesus everywhere we go. The disciples went out and obeyed the Great Commission and that's why we're here today, 2,000 years later because they were bold and obedient."

Here it was, Friday night, almost midnight, and these eager young people were gathered around me, longing to hear more, instead of desiring to party in nightclubs.

"Okay, Pastor Sonny, so we have a vision, so we evangelize, what then?" they wanted to know.

"We teach them, just like we're doing right now. We take time to disciple and teach the Word of God."

"Man, that's hard! I can't even understand the Bible," blurted Robert.

"No, not yet," I said, "But the Word of God says the Holy Spirit will teach you His Word as you read it and study it. We also learn by absorbing from the lives of our leaders; then we must get out and learn by doing the work of the ministry. Each one of us has to make an effort to be equipped so we can impart to others. If we ever stop growing, learning, and giving to others, we will die! In 2 Timothy 3:15, we're told to: 'Study to show thyself approved unto God. A workman that needeth not to be ashamed, but rightly dividing the Word of truth.'"

"If you kids are really going to be effective. You have to have the right goals and vision, and the timing needs to be right. Some of you God may want here and there are those of you that He might sent to Africa or some other foreign place. We must always be sensitive to the Holy Spirit so we go when the harvest is ready."

"That sure makes sense," Donna commented.

"Always preach the Word of God for it gives life, boldness, confidence, victory over sin, and a burden for souls. This will keep you established in Christ as well as those you win to Him."

"Pastor Sonny, you have really given us a challenge tonight. Man, I really want to be that kind of person," David said.

I could see that these young people were seriously evaluating their commitments to the Lord; they were beginning to count the cost.

We ended the meeting that night by gathering in a circle and praying. As they lifted their praises unto God, His presence was overwhelming.

Who would ever have thought that out of this group, great leaders were being formed.

We were at the school auditorium for about two years, when it became obvious that we were overstaying our welcome there, as they told us, very abruptly, that we needed to get out. Because there was no place we knew of to move, Julie and I were overwhelmed. Where would we go? How would we do it? To make matters worse we had a deadline, a date set of when we would be holding our last meeting at the school.

I gathered my ministerial staff together and said, "We've got to pray. Where in the world are we going to find a building that we can rent that will hold our large congregation? We can't go back to St. Louis Street, we've come too far for that. We've simply got to pray and believe that God is going to open up a door."

I looked and looked, but there was no place. I couldn't find a single place where we could have our service. No church was available — nothing.

There was a nightclub in our end of the town called the International Club, and I had heard that there was a possibility that the owners would sell. My curiosity got the best of me, so I went to look it over. We had no money but I wanted to see it, anyway. I went to the building and asked the owner if they were willing to sell it, and what would be the asking price. Very quickly he said, "Nine hundred thousand."

They had a bar, and were still having dances there. It was quite a popular place. I knew it would be impossible to use this for church services, so I simply decided to leave and ask no further questions. As I was pushing the door open to walk out, the Spirit of God said, "Why don't you go back in there and ask the owner if he would lease the building to you just for Sunday services."

I stopped abruptly and questioned, "Could a place like this be used for the Lord?" Still, I wanted to be obedient, so I turned around and went back in. I found the owner again and asked, "By the way, would you consider renting this place to us for Sunday services? We wouldn't require the building any other time."

He paused for a moment, rubbing his chin, then answered, "Yes, I think we could work something out." I stayed there and we discussed it back and forth, and he eventually came up with the figure that they would lease this huge building to us for $1,000 a Sunday.

I went home and called the church leadership together and told them of the proposal. We debated about it, and then decided perhaps we could look at it. I said to them, "Have you heard of the International Club?"

Everyone seemed to have heard of it, so we went to see it. The entire group was impressed with the possibilities of the building, and after everyone else left, Saul, Stella, Julie, and I stayed talking outside. The sun was going down and the light on the nightclub began to flash on and off, "Dance Tonite, Dance Tonite, Dance Tonite."

"Pastor Sonny," said Stella, "meeting in a well-known nightclub is really going to be different, but the leaders seem to be really excited."

Then Saul said, "Yeah, especially when you think about having Sunday morning service in a place that has a dance on Saturday night."

The "Nightclub"

"We are the Church," I said. "The people who love God. It's not the building. We could have church anywhere. Once we bring Jesus in, any place becomes holy ground. The building itself doesn't mean a thing." We looked at each other and then looked at the flashing neon sign, and a mixed feeling of anticipation and joy overwhelmed us.

Julie said, "Just think, every Sunday we'll be converting this dance hall into a church."

The very last Sunday in the auditorium I stood

behind the pulpit and asked the congregation if they had heard of the International Club, and I saw nods of "Yes," all over the place. I said to them, "Well, that's good. Because next Sunday we are going to have church in the International Club, and I want you to tell everybody you can."

Things really began to happen at the nightclub. We had lots more room than we did in the school auditorium, where we didn't have rooms for Sunday school, or for the different types of people that were coming to church. Here we had room galore.

We covered the bottles of liquor stacked above the bar with sheets, but even though we cleaned the whole room thoroughly, it still smelled of liquor.

It was during our time at the International Club that a strong leadership was raised up, especially as we focused on teaching to build depth in our people. That's when I also started teaching and preaching expository messages. We began a leadership training course that took place there also. We expanded our home Bible fellowships. We started Christian education classes. It was then that we as a church developed tremendous unity, leadership, and love.

It was a giant stepping stone for us as God was preparing us for what He had up ahead by solidifying and developing leadership. We continued to have conferences there also. The sheer joy of having parking spaces for everybody was a real relief. It wasn't the most attractive building, but we grew, and we were reaching the lost for Christ.

Raul and David, the two brothers who had gotten saved and discipled in our church, were beginning to take on more responsibility. When there was a vacancy in one of our churches in Riverside, we agreed that Raul should go.

After a year of pastoring as a single, he was married to a girl named Gina. David and his wife, Donna, stayed on at the parent church with me and continued to faithfully labor for the Lord.

One day before our conference, I got a call from Ed and Mitzi. "Pastor Sonny, our church in San Jose is really growing. It's bigger than when you visited last month. It's packed out with young people. I have a couple of guys I'm discipling and training, and I believe that these young men and their wives are ready to go out and take a city. They're filled with zeal for God. We've been praying and we believe the Lord has put Sacramento and Stockton on our hearts."

"Mando and Arline were up here and led us in a three-day revival. During the day, they gave classes on marriage and the home. It was awesome! A lot of people got saved and marriages were healed."

As we continued the conversation, the realization of what was taking place hit me! The multiplication was taking place—our spiritual children were continuing to go out of the parent church and now even some of their baby churches were beginning to give birth!

During this time, we held conferences twice a year. Everyone would come to the parent church, and we'd rent the nightclub for the entire week. The highlight of the week-long conference was always the last night, when the couples that were being launched out to other cities were introduced. They came up to the platform along with their sending pastors. Before we prayed and laid hands on them, they give a brief testimony.

Cal beamed, as Tony took the microphone on the last night of one particular conference. His son in the faith, Tony Guzman, was being prayed for and sent out of the San Bernardino church to San Diego. Tony, a serious and determined young man, had been discipled by Cal for several years.

Tony had been a junkie in Imperial Valley, California. After a bout with the law, he was sent to Patton State Mental Hospital for a period of two years. Upon his release, he found himself sitting on a park bench, disillusioned with life. That day, someone invited him to go to Victory Outreach in San Bernardino.

Tony gave his life to Christ and after a few years, he married a young girl from his hometown, named Nellie. He soon became the director of the rehab program and four years later joined Cal, as his associate pastor.

Tony began to feel stirred to open a church in San Diego, and shared his desire with Cal. Now, after years of discipleship and preparation, he was being sent out.

As Tony began to speak, a silence hushed the audience. With a humble and broken voice, he said, "I thank God because He raised me from the dead. Jesus has given me life, and now He's allowing me to impart life. I feel very unworthy for this task. Pastor Sonny, the rest of the leadership, thank you for believing in me. I'm planning to preach the simple, powerful gospel of God's love to everyone that I meet. I know the responsibility of pioneering a third generation church. Pastor Sonny, just like you imparted the power of the gospel to Cal and he imparted it to me, I am going to the city of San Diego and believe for the worst criminals and prostitutes to be set free. I am proclaiming it everywhere I go that there is power in the blood of Jesus and that only He can break the chains of bondage!"

That night, other young couples gave a brief testimony. One couple in particular made a tremendous impact because until this point, our churches were being planted fairly close to home. A young ex-gang member, named Rick, and his precious wife, Jeannie, took the microphone. "I thank God for saving a good-for-nothing like me and placing a call on my life. I am grateful, because even while I was in darkness and a worthless gang leader, the Lord loved me. Today I have a cause; I have a purpose, and I know I'm a person of destiny. The Lord has called me and my wife to the city of Chicago."

You could hear the gasps of the audience. He was

going two thousand miles away. "I know I'll be going far away from home, but..." his voice broke as tears streamed down his face. He continued, "We've got to heed to the calling of God. I am willing to lay down my life and pay whatever price I need to pay to get the job done!"

As I looked into the audience, I could see that Rick's testimony stirred many hearts. I noticed Raul and David along with his wife, Donna, were deeply touched.

I leaned over to Saul and said, "The Lord is going to be sending many of these kids to different parts of the world. The vision is becoming world-wide."

Saul nodded his head in agreement, "Yeah, Pastor Sonny, the future of our ministry lies with our youth. They must heed the call."

Six months later, the young men began talking about once again expanding our vision. They were feeling a call of God to go into different states and different cities. But now, all of a sudden, the Lord was taking us beyond the United States, and across the international border, into Mexico City.

There was a young man who was converted in our ministry, whom the Lord began dealing with about going into Mexico City and beginning a Victory Outreach Center. We all prayed and I sent him out and he started a work over there. Now we had gone beyond the United States. The work grew there and became successful.

From Mexico City, a work started in Zacatecas. We

started having conferences in Mexico City because all of them couldn't come to our conference in the United States. We preached and challenged the people to see that the Lord's vision was not only in the United States, but now He was taking us, for the first time, across the international borders.

Soon we were able to see the different families and many young people getting saved. We gave them the challenge that they were to take Mexico for Jesus. All those people were getting stirred up in the conferences and began to reproduce themselves, and to concentrate on reaching Mexico.

We knew we couldn't stay in the International Club forever, because the owner wanted to sell it, but he was asking too much money. At first he said, "Sonny, I'll sell it to you for nine hundred thousand." When I went back to him he said, "No, I want more than that." I knew there was something wrong, somehow it just wouldn't click, and it wasn't going to work.

Chapter Fifteen

The School

Julie and I, with some of the leaders of the church, went to see a high school complex that was built on fifteen acres. It was in the heart of La Puente, California. Our Realtor told us that it was going to be sold at auction.   We all knew for certain that we had to have the absolute mind of God if we were going to make a bid for a purchase. This would be taking a step of faith involving hundreds of thousands of dollars. We were not really afraid of doing anything as long as we knew it was the will of God.

The Lord knew that we certainly needed a permanent place in which to meet. Our people hardly knew from week to week if we'd still have a place to worship.

When we went to look at the school and surrounding grounds, it was almost a disaster. The buildings had been empty for several years and were in desperate need of repair. Instead of lawns, there were weeds everywhere, over six feet tall. Some of our people simply could not envision this ever being a place of worship, however, the fifteen acres were priceless.

The next day, just Julie and I returned to walk over the school grounds. I looked at the vastness of the property and thought, I wonder if this is the land God *has for us; it seems to be a perfect location. With some hard work it just may be suitable for a church.*

Almost as if Julie could read my mind, she asked, "Well, Sonny, what do you think?"

I paused and slowly looked around again. It was so desolate. Almost all the buildings had been vandalized. Again I thought, *Why do we always have to get things the hard way?* Words of faith suddenly began to pour forth. "Julie, we have to go to the Lord and ask if this is the place He has for us. It may seem like an impossible task for us to buy it, clean and rebuild it, but our Lord specializes in making something out of nothing!"

Both Julie and I had stepped out in faith before and knew if the Lord wanted us to have that school and property, it would be ours.

Julie went to the mountains with some of the women of the church. They were going there to fast and pray until they heard from God.

They were praying and Julie was lying on the floor face down, when one of the girls walked over to her and just stood there. Finally she said, "Julie, as I was praying, God said that I should give you this Scripture: 'Go through the camp and tell the people, Get your supplies. Three days from now you will cross the

Jordan here to go in and take possession of the land the Lord your God is giving you for your own'" (Josh. 1:7).

They continued praying and soon all of them felt that it was God's will that we purchase and possess the school. Julie came home full of confidence and reassurance. The men and I had been fasting and praying and also felt that we should go and bid. We were assured that God was with us, and that He was going to lead us. The day of the auction I felt that Julie should go and do the bidding.

Julie:

"Sonny, are you sure that you want me to do the bidding? What is our highest bid?" I asked.

"Yes, I am certain. Try not to go over two million, okay? I'll send Mitchell, Saul, and Kathy with you. I really feel this is of God," he responded.

So we went. When we arrived, I was surprised there were others who were going to bid. When I discovered it was a church we were in competition with, it really bothered me. But then I said boldly, "I am certain it is God's will for us to possess this land. We must not leave here without making the highest bid."

When the auctioneer stood up, everything got quiet as he gave the legal description of the land and the buildings. When he finished, he said, "Who will give me a million three? A million three. Do I hear a million three?"

As I was sitting there, I knew we didn't have any

money. Just the reassurance that God said, "Yes," was all we had. I looked at the auctioneer and said, "One million, three hundred twenty-five thousand," and then the other church came back with another five thousand and then I would bid another five thousand. From then on when I wanted to bid, he just looked at me and I nodded. The bidding went back and forth, up to twenty-five thousand at a time. Finally, I heard him say, "One million, four hundred thousand," and I thought my heart would burst. I could feel my whole body shaking.

Saul had his arm around my shoulders and was trying to calm me and hold me to keep me from trembling so much, because the other people who were bidding were right behind me. I tried to keep my composure, but my whole body continued to shake. I knew Sonny and the church were praying for me. I kept nodding my head and the bid went up to 1.6 million, then 1.65 million. When it reached that point, Saul leaned over and said, "Julie, don't go over two million." Still trembling, I whispered, "I'll try."

The other people suddenly said, "Can we stop the bidding for a minute?"

They got up, walked out, and conferred with each other, then returned and said, "Our bid stops at one million, six hundred ninety-five thousand dollars."

The auctioneer looked at me, waiting to see if I would raise the bid. Here I was, a girl who just a few years ago worried about paying thirty-two dollars a month rent in the projects, suddenly shouting, "One million, seven hundred thousand!"

"Going once, going twice, sold! Sold to Victory Outreach for one million, seven hundred thousand. Congratulations Victory Outreach! The fifteen acres in La Puente are yours."

I looked at Mitchell, Saul, and Kathy excitedly and shouted, "It's ours! It's ours!" Not fully realizing that I had just committed the ministry to a debt of 1.7 million dollars.

When we returned I was drained! Sonny, of course, had been praying. "Well, did we get it?" he asked.

"We got it! We got it!" I said as I jumped around a bit.

"How much?" he asked.

"One point seven million," I responded.

Sonny's face dropped and his eyes stared into space.

"One point seven million dollars! Wow, that's faith."

"Julie," I said, "The Lord is definitely leading us, and somehow He is gonna provide."

I knew God had spoken to us and I was certain He would supply our needs but I had no idea how He was going to do it!

We already had the Hacienda on the market and had been trying to sell it for about two years. However, we never had a buyer.

The man who owned the property really appreciated what we were doing and wrote us into his will. He suddenly died and we were informed his wishes were that the debt on the property be forgiven. We felt really bad when he died because he was a wonderful person.

Soon after we took the step of faith, the Hacienda sold for several hundred thousand more than we had paid for it. We still had to come up with more money. I knew God wanted me to raise the money within the church. I said to the congregation, "We have a building program going on and we need sacrificial giving. We need the spirit of sacrifice to fall on us. We must all give with a willing heart — what in the natural would seem totally impossible, with God's help, I know we can do."

They didn't seem to understand I was trying to say we needed to get that property. Somehow I was not getting the message across. One Sunday morning when I was up on the platform, I started sharing again about the need to claim that land. We all needed to give sacrificially. I got so involved, so touched, that I felt like the Lord was telling me, "Sonny, what about you, are you ready to sacrifice? Are you willing to give up your own home, so that you can get this property?"

I responded an immediate "Yes, if you want it, Lord, it's yours. Everything I own is yours." Then I spontaneously said, "I believe so much God wants us to have this land, that I'm willing to take my house, sell it, and give the money for the property. Julie and I will move back into one of the rehab houses with our family."

I then looked at Julie in front of the whole congregation and asked her, "Julie, are you willing to do that?"

There was a silence for a couple of seconds, while she fought back tears, then she said, "Yes... I'm willing."

When that happened, something broke in the congregation and the Spirit of God took over. Then Ben and Ruby got up and said, "If the pastor is willing to do that, then we're willing to give up our house and give the money to the church."

Another said, "I'm willing to give up my house, too."

Again we heard, "I'm willing to get a loan on my house."

A spirit of liberality broke loose and people began to give generously. We stood there crying in absolute joy at what God was doing. "Pastor, you don't have to sell your house. I'm gonna get a loan."

Then another said, "I have a savings account that nobody knows about." They started responding so generously that I said a prayer of gratitude in my heart to the Lord, "Thank you for giving me these humble and sensitive people. They have proven today how much they love you. Truly, he that has been forgiven much loveth much."

That's the way we were able to get the money to purchase that property.

We still had to raise more money before they would let us move in. We couldn't have services until we put in a parking lot and made some improvements. We had to raise another 800 thousand dollars to make it decent enough so that we could start having services.

To this very moment, I can't logically say how we did it, but somehow we did and we went ahead. The people made sacrifices beyond belief.

Many today have a hard time believing that God still performs miracles. They say that ended centuries ago. I want to tell you that simply isn't so and Victory Outreach is proof positive.

The Lord took us from a small church in one of the worst ghettos to this—a world outreach. When we started we were a church of addicts on welfare with little hope of ever becoming anything. God, however, elevated us to where we could purchase church property worth more than three million dollars and He has kept supplying the funds for its upkeep.

As soon as we started talking about sacrifice, some of the congregation's churchy people, the spectators, abandoned us. We lost a few hundred folks right away. *Disappeared.* The tithe didn't drop because the faithful ones put forth extra effort. Emotionally, it affected me because I felt abandoned and I was being criticized for talking about raising money. "How could he go into such a big project like that? Who does he think he is?"

I went through a whole lot of changes and had to be strong. It was about a year before we could get on the property. We were paying rent at the International Club plus raising money so we could get into our new church.

All during that time we had a prayer chain praying every day. We had groups of people praying on the land, where the parking lot was going to be. We would pray, "Lord, You know this parking lot needs to be here. We see it by faith. Lord, we need a miracle."

We'd walk all around the property asking God for everything that we knew that we needed there.

It was simple faith. We would go into the sanctuary and say, "Right here's where the pulpit's gonna be! "

Today, that's exactly where the pulpit is. It was child-like trust in our Heavenly Father. He totally came through!

One Sunday morning, after months of sacrificial giving, our people once again responded in an unbelievable manner. I realized as never before that these ex-drug addicts, prostitutes, alcoholics, welfare recipients, and what many people would call a subculture, were some of God's most committed and obedient servants on the face of the earth.

As the offering plate was passed, men and women alike started taking off their wedding bands, engagement rings, earrings, and any other jewelry of value. The men willingly gave their gold chains and bracelets. One man handed me a bracelet valued at ten thousand dollars. He told me, "Pastor, this is the most valuable possession that I ever had. It was given to me after winning a boxing championship."

I stepped up to the microphone and said to the

people, "You can't do this, it's too much. It's more than God requires of anyone."

The offering plates continued to be passed and the jewelry and gold and silver kept coming forth. I couldn't help but remember the children of Israel when Moses made the appeal for them to give for the building of the tabernacle.

"Both men and women came, all who were willing-hearted. They brought to the Lord their offerings of gold, jewelry — earrings from their fingers, necklaces, and gold objects of every kind" (Exod. 35:22). Then in Exodus we read, "But finally the workmen all left their task to meet with Moses and told him, 'we have more than enough materials on hand now to complete the job!' So Moses sent a message throughout the camp announcing that no more donations were needed. Then at last, the people were restrained from bringing more!" (Exod. 36:4-7).

Here were God's people, my precious congregation, who were also once slaves to sin and in bondage, giving their gold, silver, and jewels to build the kingdom of God, so that others could know and serve Jesus Christ, whom they had grown to love and serve.

Chapter Sixteen

New Adventures of Ministry

It was exciting walking over the property and envisioning what God had in mind. "Julie," I said, "this big room will make a wonderful fellowship hall where our people can eat, pray, and just get to know each other. Even the men from the rehab homes will enjoy this."

I knew what Julie was thinking. As I looked at the condition of the room, it needed a lot of fixing up. As a matter of fact, the entire complex was in pathetic shape. Vandalism had taken its toll. Some of the classrooms had even been burned.

The Lord gave us a wonderful idea of getting teams of people to each take one of the thirty rooms and fix it up. The worst ones would be assigned to a team with carpenters. The team would be responsible for purchasing the material and doing the work.

It was incredible to watch them take on the projects and do them so well. What a contrast to the early years on Gless Street.

As everyone labored in love, we could see the transformation taking place before our very eyes. We even developed a ball field where today over five hundred kids play ball. A kitchen was built that serves food to hundreds each day and the fellowship room is full of people learning how to relate to one another. Many of our treasures have never been to a restaurant or out of the city of Los Angeles.

The bookstore, the offices, and classrooms soon became a beautiful reality as one by one they were finished. The excitement and praise continued to grow daily as we worked on the sanctuary that would seat fifteen hundred people. Finally, the day came that we were to move in and dedicate the "church." About two hundred of us had worked until the wee hours of that Sunday morning getting the final work completed.

Julie and I thought it would surely be a time of Jubilee and celebration. As the people poured in, they were awed into near silence. Frankly, we were nearly overwhelmed with God's provision and goodness to all of us.

Everyone could sense the awesome presence of God's spirit. When I stood behind the pulpit to preach, the blanket of the Holy Spirit filled the building. I started preaching, "My precious brothers and sisters..." The power of God was on me. I turned and said to one of the men, "Could we please have the lights dimmed?"

I turned back facing the congregation and continued, "I believe that we should give this morning to Jesus in praise, prayer, and worship. We have so much to be thankful for..."

The tears welled up in my eyes, and unable to speak, I slowly surveyed the congregation. I still sensed the uniqueness of God's presence. There they sat, hundreds of former drug addicts, and gang members whom God had delivered; I saw prostitutes who now sat before me as virgins in Christ; mothers who had come pleading for their sons; the couples who were willing to sell their homes to get this property.

My eyes then rested on my family. My children whom we had nearly sacrificed for this moment in their lives; and my wife who had endured every conceivable hardship in the desert, so that we could enter this promised land. I looked at all the men and women. Those people had given freely their gold, bracelets, engagement rings, jewelry, coins, and dollars for us to be here. This was no the time for preaching. This was our moment to worship God and praise Him, for we had crossed over Jordan, and we had finally arrived.

I thought we were going to dance unto the Lord, but all most of us did was cry. We were all so grateful for finally arriving at the "Promised Land."

The service was very solemn and meaningful. It set

the scene for the future and for what God had in mind. The facilities were so large that at first we felt it would take years to fill, but God had other plans.

He began to give me a burden for the drug and gang-infested black communities. Daily, as I heard news reports, and read the newspapers, my heart would be kindled. The dealing of coke and crack, the senseless killings, I knew if Jesus was walking on the earth bodily, this is where He would be.

He wouldn't move away to the suburb and forget about those in sin and bondage. We had a few black brothers attending our churches and several had graduated from our rehab program. At one of our conferences in front of over six thousand in attendance, the Lord impressed me to call up all the black brothers and sisters who were ex-dopers, prostitutes, and gang members. Several hundred responded and we began to pray. As we did, a prophecy came forth. "Just as the Lord has delivered you, my black brothers and sisters from the bondage of sin, the Lord has many in the cities of America who need to know that Jesus is alive and able to set them free."

"God is going to give us a breakthrough in the black ghettos. Revival is coming to those who are blind and in darkness."

From that time, a tremendous breakthrough began to take place in the black communities.

The work continued to expand so rapidly that the

need for training was of utmost importance. We had been praying for some time about the Lord, sending us someone to take over the school of ministry. Robert was a young man who had come to us on a court commitment when a murder charge was dropped due to insufficient evidence. He had a real desire to learn, so he studied several years and earned a degree from Southern California College. He responded to the need of teaching the Word of God and began to develop our Victory Outreach School of Ministry. We wanted a curriculum tailor-made to meet the needs of our ministry.

Robert was also pioneering a church in West L.A., so his labors were split in two. We began to pray for someone who could work full-time to help train and develop leaders and potential leaders.

The Lord sent a single young man who had grown up in Wichita, Kansas, by the name of Doug Hollis. He was a student at Fuller Theological Seminary. In his senior year, he came to Victory Outreach to study our leadership training model. He also had attended our conference and visited our church. Soon he became aware that we needed someone to take over the school of ministry. He then called and asked to meet with me.

"Pastor Sonny," Doug said, "shortly after getting involved with Victory Outreach, I heard you speak for the first time. As I listened, I heard my heart beat in another person. I've been studying you for some time and I'm convinced you really care for people, and I see you really believe in them. You have a heart to go anywhere and do anything to reach a hurting person."

As he shared, I felt funny hearing someone speak to me about what he had observed in me, but I could see he was sincere. He continued, "Pastor, you represent what is in the depths of my spirit. I'll never forget going to the altar after you spoke. I wept and wept. I'll never forget it. At that moment it was like it was branded on my heart, the fact that there are other people with the same kind of vision that I have.

"I, too, believe in people and I want to take part in what you are doing helping these guys and girls rise to their potential."

My heart leaped inside when I realized the Lord had brought this young "square" intellectual to help further develop our school of ministry.

God really opened the door for Doug. Our people responded beautifully to him and our school began to blossom from just a few students into the hundreds. We started extensions and in a short time, had over a thousand students involved. People were hungry for evangelistic training and growth, which is a true sign of revival.

Julie:

Another exciting thing began to take place. We realized that our women needed special training because many were expressing a desire to be used of God.

We began having United Women's Services, uniting all of our churches. I'd invite outside speakers, looking for women with a strong, uncompromising, biblical message.

One time, I went to hear a well-known speaker. I went with the intention of inviting her to come and be of help to us. She spoke simply, but beautifully, about prayer and walking in communion with God.

I waited after the service so I could speak to her about coming and sharing with our women. "I know you must be a very busy person," I said, "but do you think it would be possible for you to come and share with our women? I get everyone in the churches together and..."

I didn't get to finish, because she interrupted me and said, "When?"

Startled, I responded, "Uh, anytime this year."

She said, "Well, my dear, that's out of the question. You see, I'm booked solid for the next three years! Write me a letter and I'll try to fit you in after that."

I walked away feeling rejected, but then I gathered my thoughts and began to re-evaluate what I was doing. The Lord had given me this vast army of women and it was not anyone else's duty but mine, to see that they were equipped.

I began to speak and challenge our pastor's wives to equip themselves to train and equip our women. I challenged them to study and prepare. They began to grow in the Word and began teaching and preaching the Word of God. Everything we needed was right there. All they needed was to be challenged and for someone to believe in them. The Lord began using many of the women. One was Arline Gonzales. He raised her to teach not only from books and written material, but with the example of her life. She taught in depth on servanthood.

The Lord began lifting up others with a desire to teach. Joesy was one that the Lord began using mightily in preaching and teaching. Mitzi, Ed's wife, began preaching the Word, stirring the hearts of young women.

Women and young girls continued coming to Christ and were being challenged to commit their lives to the Lord's service. The women began to get stirred up about world evangelism. They began fund-raising efforts and today are largely responsible for the world missions budget that runs into the hundreds of thousands. Through their united efforts they began buying vehicles, literature, instruments, and many of the needed tools to reach a foreign country. Many of our single girls responded to the call of God on their lives and began going to different countries to give of their services on the foreign fields. Some help in children's church, others in evangelism and office work. Some run our women's rehabilitation homes with the goal of training and discipling a local girl to eventually take it over.

One such girl is Deete. Deete is a young girl who was

delivered from a life of heroin addiction. Upon graduating from our rehab home, she felt a call to the mission field in Barcelona, Spain. Here is an excerpt from a recent letter:

Dear Pastor Sonny and Julie,

God is faithful. He's given us a breakthrough in the women's home. The few women we have are staying, growing, and very teachable. Last month, the church prayed for our first women's leader in the home. Her name was Maria Jesus. She came in weighing less than sixty pounds, with no desire to live. Before my eyes, I saw a lifeless woman healed. Her husband is in the men's home.

Pastor Nulberto performed his first wedding with this precious couple. I had the privilege of being her maid of honor. Now Maria Jesus, our first fruit, has gone to be with the Lord. She died of a heart attack. The majority of drug addicts here have AIDS, and the hospitals here lack concern. I had taken Maria Jesus for a blood transfusion and her heart rejected the type of blood they gave her.

Pastor Nulberto and her husband took her body back to her family in Aligante, Spain. They hadn't seen her in four years and were comforted to know she wasn't on drugs and had given her life to the Lord. Now, they want a Victory Outreach Church and a women's home in Aligante.

Pastor Nulberto had the privilege to minister to many and we also brought home Maria Jesus' sister, a notorious dope addict from Aligante.

Pastor Sonny and Julie, I am committed to intense discipling and imparting the vision that God has called us to. Simple, basic, practical things with lots of prayer, the Word, and servanthood. I feel the task He has for me is just beginning. My desire, burden, and vision is to build solid women of prayer.

I love you,

Deete

Through much prayer and intense teaching of the Word of God, many of the young, married women also began growing and developing a strong desire to be everything our Lord has called them to be.

Throughout the years, we came to realize that the wife of a servant of God can either enhance his ministry or tear it down. I committed myself to teach and disciple the wives of future leaders. This has become one of my priorities in life.

After a Sunday morning service, David and Donna came up to me. I could see that they were anxious to tell me something.

"Pastor Sonny," David said, "we know you have

always prayed for someone to go to New York City, and I also have prayed for the Lord to raise someone. Well, last night before going to sleep, as Donna and I knelt to pray we felt a call to New York City. I always thought I should stay and minister here. Our church has grown so much, but I can see God raising up others like Charlie and his wife Pogie."

Donna said, "Yes, like David said, I didn't think we'd ever leave our church and our family, but last night as we prayed, we felt the Lord telling us it was time for us to go and pioneer a work. For a long time, we both have felt a burden for New York City."

As they continued sharing, I prayed a prayer of thanksgiving in my heart thanking the Lord for raising the right couple for my city. The Lord in His sovereignty had raised a young couple who had to rely solely and completely on the Lord. Now they were the ones who were being sent to a foreign city to a new people.

I knew, just as the Lord had worked His miracles through me in Los Angeles, they were going to be the instruments to bring revival on the streets of New York City. When they left, the Lord continued to raise up young men and women and the work continued to expand.

Sonny inviting a gang to a "gang rally."

Victory Outreach Church, LaPuente.

Chapter Seventeen

Restoring the Fallen

One of the hardest and most disappointing aspects of the ministry is when one of your members or pastors backslides. In the beginning of the ministry, this has happened much more than I like to admit. It was always such a wonderful experience and joy to see God move in a life and free a person from sin. The joy was unspeakable to then watch them grow and turn into firebrands for the Lord and in the knowledge of God and His Word.

Then, suddenly, like a lightening bolt, some would lose it and return to the things of the world. There were many times Satan would tell me that the ministry was in vain, "Eventually, all of them will return to the drugs and me. Victory Outreach won't keep them."

When Ray stepped into our house, I knew at once there was something wrong. I put my hand on his shoulder and asked, "Ray, are you all right?"

"No, Pastor Sonny, I can't make it one more day. I've messed up and I can't ever imagine myself serving God again," Ray said in anguish.

These were cries from one of my sons in the faith. Ray had served the Lord faithfully for sixteen years. The Lord had used him mightily as a youth leader, then as the pastor of a thriving church. He had also been blessed with a beautiful wife named Gina.

"What do you mean, Ray? The Lord is a forgiving God and is here to forgive you," I pleaded.

"Not with what I've done. I've sinned against God. I've disappointed you and brought disgrace to Victory Outreach. Pastor Sonny, I've reverted back to my old ways. I'm drinking and have even started using cocaine again," Ray put his face in his hands and began to sob.

"Ray, listen to me," I almost commanded. "There is no sin that God won't forgive."

Ray lifted his head as he sobbed, saying, "I've even pulled a few armed robberies. Gina is in the hospital, where she just gave birth to our first son. Pastor, she named him Raymond. I told her not to, but she did anyway. I feel so ashamed and unworthy."

My heart was breaking and I knew that the Lord was feeling Ray's pain as well. Ray was either going to be restored or destroyed completely by the enemy. I also felt for his lovely wife, Gina, who was a precious, soft-spoken girl. I placed my arm around him and prayed. I came against the enemy, who was trying to destroy my son in the faith. I prayed that the Lord would restore him and forgive Ray and cleanse him of his sin.

As I continued praying, I asked the Lord to give Ray an abundance of His grace. I stood there wondering, how can this be? Ray fall? He had gone through some severe trials recently, but I also knew he had faced bigger ones in the past. I had always considered him a strong warrior, and he was the last one that I would have ever worried about falling.

While Ray and Gina were having a barbecue at their home, a young girl from their church had drowned in the swimming pool. This incident, along with financial problems were overwhelming, especially so because Ray had neglected his time alone with God. He tried carrying the weight of the ministry by himself instead of taking his burdens to the Lord. Because of this, he slowly began to turn back to his old ways.

After we prayed, Ray said, "Pastor, I know that God wants me to turn myself in to the police. However, I feel that there are a few things that I must take care of first."

The next day, Gina was released from the hospital and came directly to our house. Julie met her at the door. She had the newborn baby in her arms and the other children were snuggled next to her. When Julie's eyes met Gina's, they both began to cry. Gina then buried her face on Julie's shoulder and cried uncontrollably. Julie took Ray's little family in the guest room.

All of them were now weeping. The children didn't quite understand what was happening, but they somehow felt the hurt and heartache in their mother.

Julie opened the Word of God and told Gina, "Listen, I know right now everything looks hopeless. One day you were a pastor's wife with friends and respect. Now today you feel downcast and alone. I want you to read with me Psalm 91:1-4, 11,12:

> He who dwells in the shelter of the Most High will rest in the shadow of the Almighty. I will say of the Lord, He is my refuge and my fortress, my God, in whom I trust. Surely, he will save you from the fowler's snare and from the deadly pestilence. He will cover you with his feathers, and under his wings you will find refuge; his faithfulness will be your shield and rampart.

> For he will command his angels concerning you to guard you in all your ways; they will lift you up in their hands, so that you will not strike your foot against a stone.

The Lord's presence was so real as He revealed His love so strongly through those verses of Scripture. Julie prayed with Gina and the children, then invited them to spend the night. In the morning we gathered around the breakfast table. Gina looked at me and said, "Pastor Sonny, I know things look impossible for me right now, the future looks bleak and hopeless; but somehow I know, that as long as I stay under the shadow of the Almighty, He will take care of me and the children."

Ray turned himself in as he said he would and the judge set a court date. We had experienced hard blows before, but somehow, when a minister like Ray takes a fall it hurts more, because it affects so many people.

I had asked Saul and Charlie, one of the staff members, to call our leadership together because I felt strongly that we had to be a restoring church and we had to make a clear stand on how to receive and deal with a fallen brother.

I began with, "Ray has taken a hard fall and he is presently in jail. He began using drugs again and even went so far as to pull an armed robbery."

One of our young leaders spoke up. "But Pastor Sonny, how can this be? Ray was a pastor. I can see him falling...but armed robbery?"

"Yes," I said, "when a person goes back to his old life the Bible says you get seven times worse and Ray did just that. I feel we should help his family until he gets out, which may take some time. Gina and the children are hurting enough as it is."

I could see that some of the young men did not agree, so I felt I should elaborate more on why we, as a church, had to agree on where to stand. I said, "It is important to know we are members of the same Body. The way to judge our relationship with God is to judge our relationship with man. In 1 John 4:20 and 21 it says, 'If a man say, I love God, and hateth his brother, he is a liar; for he that loveth not his brother whom he hath seen, how can he love God whom he hath not seen? And this commandment have we from him, that he who loveth God loves his brother also.'

"That is the way that God approaches everything. The standard of how intimate your relationship is with God, the invisible relationship, is measured by how intimate your relationships are with man. When a person falls, instead of kicking him, we should go to them, lift them up, and do all that we can to restore them back to God and their ministry. We don't have to justify their sin, but we sure can give them support and let them know that we love them unconditionally. God forgives those who forgive others, too."

"Pastor Sonny," one of them said, "isn't that like saying, 'go ahead and sin, it's okay?' Perhaps we are in danger of compromising our stand against sin."

I continued with no comment. "It is important for Christians to know that we are members of the same Body. For example: when you stub your toe on a stone, you don't spank your toe for getting stubbed. You don't gouge your eyes out because your eyes didn't see the stone. You use medication or sutures or whatever the hurt toe needs to restore it to health and keep it from hurting.

"A sore toe, once healed, can bring blessing to the rest of the body. However, a toe that is cut off can never help you again. The same is true of a brother or sister in Christ who has fallen if they are rejected and not restored.

"During some of the Christian TV scandals, the Christian church had the attention of the world through national TV and we failed miserably with statements like these: 'They are cancers that need to be removed from the body of Christ.' 'They are getting what they deserve.' 'Let them resign? We have already thrown them out!' 'They should be stoned.' 'They are disgusting.'

"The list could go on and on as we Christians publicly picked their bones. The world watched and scoffed at us as we ripped, slandered, and tore at one another. This should have been a time of forgiveness, tough love, and restoration. But instead, the world saw us fight, slander, hate, and seek revenge. Shame on us and God help us!"

Saul interrupted, "Men, the Bible tells us of many leaders who have fallen and how they were restored. God is not calling perfect people to serve Him. He is calling sinners like us! He forgave us and transformed us so that we can serve Him and be an example of His transforming power and not our own self-righteousness and goodness. When we batter down someone who has fallen, we are most likely trying to show the world how good we are who didn't fall. We are flaunting our self-righteousness instead of the righteousness and grace of Jesus Christ."

"You're right Saul," I said continuing. "All of us need

to be on our faces before the Lord seeking His help to live godly lives. The Church must conduct itself in such a way that those, especially ministers, who fall into sin can come and confess, get help, and be restored."

I could see the Lord was doing a work in all of us. The spirit of God united our decision as we prayed and the love of God filled all of us in the room.

I later expressed to the entire church body, "In the last few years we've seen brothers in the Lord fall away. When they've wanted to repent and come back to God, we as a Church did not reach out and embrace them.

"I want our church to be a place of refuge. I want the love of God to flow through you and me so that the healing of God's Holy Spirit will help us to embrace our brother who is weak or fallen. We will not compromise with sin, but if a brother repents, we must restore him."

Our congregation began responding to the challenge of restoration. When people returned who were backslidden or hurting, our people didn't ask questions. They prayed with them and even began inviting them over for dinner and loving them back into the kingdom of God.

When Ray was released after over a year in jail, our Church, by then, was ready to receive him. Ray, however, had a hard time receiving their love because he felt so unworthy. Slowly, the love of God won out. Today, several years later, Ray and Gina are on my ministerial staff fully restored. They reach out to people with similar problems, taking them into their home and spending countless hours sharing the love of God and restoring their broken, wounded lives.

Only the Lord can make a tragedy into a blessing. These last years we have seen many pastors and leaders restored fully knowing and understanding that, "All things work together for good to those that love God and are called according to his purpose" (Rom. 8:28).

Chapter Eighteen

The International Vision

Our international vision first began with Mexico then expanded to Europe. After a few months of being in our new church property, Julie and I were again invited to go to England, and this time a group from Holland requested we visit them as well. Our tour of England was explosive as hundreds responded to the gospel. When we finished there we went to Holland.

At our first street rally in the city of Arnhem, the brethren who invited us had built a platform in the middle of the town square. The crowd was huge and consisted mostly of young people. The rally was held on a Friday night and many of those at the square were drinking and disorderly. The crowd was so keyed up, that they mercilessly heckled a singing group off the platform.

As I preached I had to speak with an interpreter and this gave them opportunity to begin to harass me. "Get out of here," they yelled.

I continued speaking but they got louder and louder. I have preached in prisons, in gang-infested areas, and in shooting galleries where junkies were fixing — these kids didn't know who they were messing with. I represented the King of kings. The Master and Creator of all, the Lord Jesus Christ.

The interpreter was terrified and asked, "Shall we stop?"

I said, "No! The Lord loves these young people and if I get killed preaching the gospel then let it be so! I can't think of a better way to go."

I continued speaking and could see Julie with a few of the women from the local church praying. The crowd got louder and began coming toward the platform. They had turned into a "raging mass of young people."

"Hey preacher, go back to America!" they screamed.

I felt the Holy Spirit as I now spoke. "I don't come to you with fancy words. But I come in the name of my Lord and Saviour Jesus. The One who set me free from heroin addiction."

That statement got their attention. As I continued speaking, I turned and looked at my interpreter, He was saying that we should go. We continued, however, speaking the Word of God with boldness. The crowd began to calm down, stopped jeering, and began to listen. Suddenly, a hush hit the crowd. There were a few hundred people in the square that night. As we gave the call to come forward to accept the living Christ as Lord and have their sins forgiven, a rush of the Holy Spirit came upon the crowd of young people and they began to respond.

They were weeping and crying unashamedly and knelt at the front of the platform in plain sight.

That was one of the most powerful manifestations of God's power I had ever witnessed.

After the meeting, as we walked toward the car, the interpreter, who was a distinguished young man, expressed to me how this had been his first experience interpreting at an outdoor evangelist crusade. He asked me, "What was that hot feeling I felt as I was interpreting? I felt as if hot oil was falling on my head."

I turned to him and said, "That, sir, was the anointing of the Holy Spirit. It is the anointing that breaks the yoke. We never attempt to go against the evils of this world without praying, fasting, and trusting God for the anointing."

"That was some experience! I have never felt anything like it, " he said. "I thought at first the crowd was going to kill me, but when that hot feeling came over me I thought it might kill me first. I still have that feeling." he said as his eyes welled up with tears.

As we continued to share about the glory of God, a young man came up to me and introduced himself. I had recognized him before in other services. "Hi, my name is Ferri. I've been following you from city to city and I want you to know I've been praying for a ministry like Victory Outreach to come to Holland. I am an ex-junkie and I know that God has sent you. You are the answer to my prayers."

Ferri was a handsome, young, dark-complexioned, Dutch-Indonesian. His eyes beamed as he spoke. "Sonny, Sonny, you've got to come see the need on our streets of Amsterdam. We need a Victory Outreach Ministry," he pleaded.

"Yes, yes, Ferri, But I can't right now," I answered.

He persisted that Julie and I go with him to the city of Amsterdam to see the need. Finally, we agreed to go the next morning and take a look at the need.

The city of Amsterdam is a beautiful, busy city with picturesque canals and people on bicycles going in every direction. Ferri arrived early in the morning to pick us up at the hotel. After a cup of Dutch coffee, we set out on our tour. Julie and I were totally unprepared for what we were about to experience.

We boarded the tram on our way to visit one of the junkie hang-outs. On the tram we sat next to three young teenagers. One of them was hitting his head against the window. I cold see he was in pain. I immediately recognized what was taking place — he needed a fix. The other two were also in pain, with agony written all over their faces. I felt compelled to talk to them. Ferri was interpreting for me as I said, "Man, I used to be a junkie, too."

They looked at me with disbelief. I rolled up my sleeve and showed them my old needle tracks. This caught their attention. I was speaking to them real fast and they were listening. It was a very emotional moment because they were suffering, yet they were doing their best to listen. The boy hitting his head on the window of the tram said, "I'm sorry, I'm sorry, keep talking to me! It's just that I'm sick and I need a fix."

They tried to listen but were sick and trembling. The boy then hit himself against the glass of the tram again. I thought he was gonna break it. I kept witnessing and sharing to them about the power of Jesus. I told them Jesus was able to set them free — that He could take the desire away for drugs and make them completely whole.

As Julie looked on, she began to cry because of the compassion she felt.

I began to pray for them in front of everyone. Although hurting and desperate, they had respect and bowed their heads. After the prayer, I quickly scribbled my United States address on a piece of paper. We arrived at their stop. As they got off the tram I pleaded with them, "If you want help, I'll help you."

"Sure, but America is so far away..." and they were gone.

On that first day, Ferri introduced us to over fifty

young people who were on hard drugs. The next day we went with him to a coffee house where his friends had gathered to meet us. In Holland, hashish and marijuana are like beer and wine in the United States. They are socially accepted by the government. Most of the coffee shops in Holland offer a soft drug menu to choose your favorite blend of marijuana or color of hash. As I talked to them, they couldn't seem to hear enough. They were just like sponges. These unsaved people gathered around us and would ask me questions and I would answer. I stayed sharing with them about the Lord till they closed the coffee shop at three in the morning.

At first they could hardly believe that I was a pastor and asked, "Are you sure that you're a pastor? Pastors over here don't do this kind of thing. You don't ever see them out here, especially at this hour of the night."

I responded, "I do this all the time in America. This is what I believe God wants me to do and I am a pastor."

It was real hard for them to believe it. "Wow, you're really a pastor? That's the kind of church I'd like to go to."

The challenge from God was burning into my spirit. The decadence of Holland was overwhelming to me. I had envisioned a land of blonde-haired girls in pigtails, white hats, and wooden shoes. The quaint windmills of Don Quixote, the tulips of bright, blazing red, and the silver skates of Hans Brinker. When Ferri took us to the red-light district of Amsterdam, I was jarred into the reality of what Satan has done to this land of fairytales.

There was block after block of buildings, two and three stories tall, with large store-front windows. These were not to sell out of, but for the passer-by to see in. Standing behind each window in full view were not mannequins, but young girls, prostitutes displaying their nearly nude bodies "for sale."

Julie and I had worked with prostitutes in the past but somehow these beautiful girls had lost all sense of dignity and self-respect. They looked as if they weren't really alive; only existing.

As we walked street after street there was the same look on every face. Their eyes displayed emptiness, hopelessness, and despair.

As we left the red-light district, Julie turned to me and said, "Sonny, I'll never forget the look in their eyes until we can come back and proclaim the gospel to them. That sad, hopeless look in their eyes will haunt me; especially when we have what they need...Jesus."

Usually when I come back from a trip like that it's all inside of me and the burden will come out in my preaching and sharing. During the conference that we had in L.A., I started sharing about the need in Holland. "Man, there's a tremendous need. There are drug addicts over there who are bound and there needs to be a Victory Outreach in Holland."

I shared about how the drug addicts were begging us, "Come and help us over here."

I told them about the young prostitutes in the windows. The need in Amsterdam was just like a Macedonian call.

Ferri kept calling me after we got back saying, "Sonny, don't forget we need a Victory Outreach here in Holland." Julie and I were thinking about going ourselves. I said to her, "Julie, maybe the Lord is calling us to go to Holland."

After much prayer we realized it wasn't for us to go. The call was for someone else. As I shared in the conference the vision of reaching the continent of Europe, young Pastor Raul listened intently.

He had been pastoring the church in Riverside, California for about two years. When he heard me speak about Holland, God began speaking to him and telling him he was supposed to go. When Raul came up to me and said, "Pastor Sonny, God has called me to go to Holland. I know without a shadow of a doubt that I am supposed to go. Both my wife and I are willing to leave our church in Riverside and step out in faith.

I had someone else in mind that I felt was probably more equipped to go. He sounded convincing. "Raul, would you want to go there and check it out first, spy out the land?" I asked.

"No," he said. "I don't have to spy out anything. I know God has called us and we are ready to go."

I told him to pray on it some more and get a confirmation that it really was the Lord. The call wouldn't leave him, and the more he prayed, the more he felt that God was calling him and his wife to Holland. He felt it hammering inside him. It was a heavy burden that wouldn't leave. I asked the church to pray. This was a big step and we needed the leading of the Holy Spirit. As Julie and I were praying, God said, "Yes!"

The day came that we laid hands upon Raul, Gina, and a team of workers and launched them out into Amsterdam. Once again, our church was given a challenge. It's one thing giving to people you can see and experience the change that takes place in their lives, but to send nine thousand dollars a month to people who most of the church will never see or know was another matter.

That didn't seem to bother our people, however, and they met the challenge, obeyed God, sacrificed even more, and gave ungrudgingly. As a matter of fact, one man felt led of God and challenged the people to give a double tithe that we could reach Amsterdam for Christ, and many did.

Raul was able to rent a place and then he began to walk the streets, without even knowing the language, or anything about the culture. This was the first time he had ever been out of the states. He just went with the vision and calling of God. He shared with me how this minister came up to him and said, "Young man, I have a piece of advice for you. If I were you, I would take my little wife and go back to the U.S., because we don't need any more missionaries over here. We have enough." Then, he actually started poking his finger at Raul's chest and told him, "We don't need more American missionaries here. Go home! That's the advice that I have for you."

Then I asked him, "How did you respond? What did you tell him?"

He said, "I felt an extraordinary anointing come over me and I received a boldness that I never had before. I said, 'Sir, I'll have you know that we're not here because we decided to come here or because it's our choice. We're here because God has called us here, and here we're gonna stay.'"

I then asked, "What did he say?"

"He just got upset and walked away," Raul told me.

Raul called and wrote often. Here is an excerpt from one of his letters:

We feel greatly challenged here in the city of Amsterdam. Being one of the most international cities in the world and considered by many to be the doorway to Europe, it is the ideal place to work for God. This city has one hundred thirteen different nationalities and forty-one major ethnic groups. The daily scene here is one of increasing violence, drugs, high unemployment, loneliness, heavy occult activity, overcrowding, and prostitution. This makes it fertile ground for the gospel!

We are excited and working hard and praying hard to see God give a great harvest.

I tell you, Pastor Sonny, my vision has really widened; we have to make disciples. I really praise the Lord for allowing us to see the things that are taking place. The need is great all around us, but we know where God has called us to and we're doing our best here. The prostitutes are open to us when we pray for them and talk about Jesus. Tears come down their faces. They are still checking us out to see if we're for real. God has been healing people that we pray for and for the first time somebody prophesied in a service. The Holy Spirit is really working with this baby church.

When we examine the work in Holland, we understand it wasn't so much that Raul was exceptionally trained, or that he had exceptional qualities. It was the right timing, the right place, the right man with the right message. We are believing God that this work will continue throughout Europe and wherever there are people who are in the pits of darkness and despair. We want to take them the message of hope.

Raul brought Nicky Cruz to Amsterdam. The crusade was a success, souls got saved, and more people came under exposure to the ministry. The church grew to over one thousand members and the ministry is still expanding. With the sacrificial giving of our people, we raised twenty-five thousand dollars as a down payment so Raul could acquire a five-story building and it has become the European training center. We are going to train believers from all over Europe there. The Amsterdam church has planted three satellite churches, and plans one in Italy soon.

The same type of people that we reach in America, inner city people, we are reaching in the cobblestoned streets of Holland. Impossible cases that have now begun to find Jesus as their Saviour. They, too, have become Treasures Out of Darkness.

From the very humble beginnings of our ministry, when I had a group of people who were all on welfare, even then God was preparing us. That is why the Lord led me to tell them that we had to live by faith and trust God so that we could be the instruments to bring blessings, not only locally, but throughout the world.

It has been thrilling for me to see the expansion going on all over the world in these last years. We have expanded not only to Holland, but all over Mexico; Sao Paulo, Brazil; London, England; Barcelona, Spain; and Togo, Africa. Other South American countries have invited our ministry to come and help their youth.

Recently, Julie took a group of women to visit some of the missions that we have in Europe. This group of women have helped Julie raise funds to support a lot of the work there, so she wanted to take them with her so that they could be more motivated and their vision could grow.

They began their tour in London, England, and stayed there for a few days with the pastor's wife. They walked the streets with the people and got to meet them. They visited Amsterdam, and then went on to Spain.

Julie:

It was so beautiful to see firsthand what God was doing in Spain through our ministry. The Lord had raised up a beautiful couple by the name of Nulberto and Marilyn to pioneer the work there.

Rafa, a precious young man in our rehabilitation home, took us down to the streets on which they were working. Already they had a few converts. Rafa was anxious to show us where he came from and where he was witnessing through the back alleys and such. The streets in Spain are really different. There are these back alleyways that are narrow, with buildings that are tilted. The architecture is beautiful; the buildings are about four hundred years old.

Rafa said, "This is a very dangerous area with a lot of crime and full of junkies. You girls look like tourists. I know you don't think you do, but you do. You had better let me take all your stuff, I know these people. I'll go before you and let them know that you are okay. But let me hold anything that's valuable."

We did what he said, and prayed for the Lord to protect us because you could feel the presence of evil. Although it was mid-day, the alleyways were dark and foreboding. The prostitutes started coming out of the bars. He gathered a lot of interest and crowds around him. He gave his testimony and then we shared the gospel and prayed for them. It was really beautiful to see that God was doing the very same thing there in Spain, as He was in L.A.

When we were on our way back on the train, I was sitting with Rafa and he told me that he had just read Sonny's autobiography, *Once a Junkie*.

"I was very touched because your husband was just like me. I want to ask you something. Tell me a little bit about the people over there. Is it true that these people are sending money to us here so this church can go on? Is it true that the parent church in the United States is supporting the pastors and that you're the ones who are supporting it?"

I said, "Yes, it's true. Not only is it true, but there are thousands of people in Victory Outreach just like you who God has saved and are working and sacrificially giving."

He asked, "Thousands of them?"

"Thousands of them are out there like you, who are making it and who are serving God. Now they're motivated to give so that you and others like you can know Jesus Christ as their Saviour."

He said, "It's so hard for me to visualize this and believe that there could be other people like me. Not only that, but that they're working, they've gotten on their feet, and that they are able to support and give so that I could be saved!"

By that time he had tears in his eyes as he continued, "I want you to do something for me. I want you to go back and tell these people who are giving that you met me. That my name is Rafa. You be sure to thank them for giving of their finances and that I am going to make it. I'm just barely getting up, getting myself strong. I'm going to get a job and start supporting the work here. Sister Julie, you will see that out of this church we're gonna be able to support the work of God all over Spain. The same vision that God has given you in the U.S., God is going to do here, and I'm going to be the beginning of it."

The report really touched my heart. Rafa had caught the vision. The Holy Spirit had revealed that to him. There are hundreds of young men like him who have now gotten jobs and are supporting the work in Spain. God truly is giving us TREASURES OUT OF DARKNESS.

Timothy, Sonny Boy, Doreen, Debbie, Sonny, & Julie

Sonny Launching Out Sonny Boy

Chapter Nineteen

THE BATTLE STILL RAGES

David and Donna had been in New York City for several years and had a rough time adjusting. David called often but the following telephone conversation was a delight and encouraging to receive.

"Pastor Sonny, we've finally had a breakthrough here in New York. Our home is full of guys and girls who have given their lives to Christ. Daily we are seeing the Lord delivering people. It's amazing that everywhere we go, people are hungry to hear about our Living Saviour."

Donna got on the phone and after giving me a warm greeting asked to speak to Julie. "Hi Julie," she said excitedly. "Finally, I can say it's really happening. Although it was difficult at first for us to adjust to the new foods and different cultures, the Lord has been faithful. It's easier for us now that Victory Outreach has churches in Philadelphia, New Jersey, Washington, DC, and in the Bronx. We have been been able to have fellowship and strengthen each other. The east coast is experiencing revival as never before.

"Julie, I'm amazed at the power that we have in Jesus. All we do is pray, fast, and take the message of the gospel to the neediest drug-infested areas we can find. As we share how Jesus is a living Saviour and able to set them free, people respond and are openly accepting Christ."

Julie then asked, "Where are you holding services?"

"We've got a nice building now and no longer meet in our living room," Donna said with excitement.

After they chatted a few minutes about the women that were coming to Christ, David got back on the phone. He began to share, "Pastor, the Lord is manifesting himself everywhere we go. In the street meetings, jail services, and on the one-to-one witnessing.

"It was a slow beginning, Pastor Sonny. During our first years we were planting seeds. Now we're beginning to reap a harvest and revival is taking place. Donna and I know we're in the right place at the right time."

Daily letters and reports from the different cities in the United States and abroad keep coming in. These young couples call and express their astonishment at the power of the gospel and how the Lord is manifesting

His power through them.

By this time, the Victory Outreach School of Ministry at the parent church in La Puente was well on its way. The leadership realized that we had to develop a training center in Europe if we were going to continue to effectively evangelize the continent. Our people there needed to be adequately equipped.

After much prayer and discussion, Doug expressed a desire to go and assist Raul in the leadership development and training. Although it was difficult to release him, we all agreed it was time.

After Doug was in Holland for a period of time, Julie and I received this letter from him:

Dear Pastor Sonny and Julie,

Greetings from Amsterdam! God is really blessing in so many ways, and I am excited just to be in the very center of His will for my life. Thank you for being so sensitive and responsive to the Spirit and for assisting and facilitating my coming over here. I have no doubt but that this is all in the sovereign plan of God and He is working out His purposes.

I will call you concerning more of this later.

I also want to really thank you sincerely from my heart for the openness with which you have always received me, for the encouragement and support that you give. But most of all for your godly example that I continually see in you — "fleshing out" the very heart of God — with all His compassion and love for people! I think that modelling has impacted me so deeply that I can never be the same. Thanks. Also, thanks for believing in me and challenging me to rise to the level of my potential in God — you've done that in so many ways — I can't thank you enough.

I really do believe that we can take the world for Jesus and I am putting my entire life behind that belief. There is an awesome and enormous world out there that really does need Jesus...but we truly have the answer and the ingredients that will make us a powerful force in touching and reaching lives in every corner of the earth!

Thanks for being obedient to God's voice and for enduring all of the hardships and trials along the way. I really love you, and believe in what we are doing together! This is just the beginning — we are going to reap the harvest! God Bless you.

Your Son in the Faith, Doug

One morning I was sitting at the kitchen table as Julie was busy fixing coffee. I was somewhat troubled with this thought, The *evangelism efforts are going too slow! The development of our leadership and pastors have to expand at a faster pace.* Up to this point our men are maturing by ministering in the home cell groups, rehab homes, prison teams, and street evangelism.

I realized that some of the men who had been sent to other cities to pioneer churches had gone out with limited experience. Many of them were having problems in various areas such as administration, developing leadership, and were limited in strategic ideas to reach their cities. I was also limited in numerical growth in my church facility...we were already into double services on Sunday morning and considering going into triple services.

I motioned for Julie to come and sit down. I knew she could tell I had been troubled. "Julie," I said, "you know how we need to continue to expand in our training of new leadership and how I'm feeling frustrated over the slow growth."

"Yes, Sonny," she responded, "but I wouldn't say it's such a slow growth. The Lord has helped us to expand all over the United States and we are beginning to have breakthroughs in foreign countries."

"I know Julie, but we have to speed up the pace. I think that if we open satellite churches within a twenty-mile radius of our church and the pastor in training continues working, supporting his family, we could have a faster expansion."

"Where would they hold services?" she asked.

"During the week they could use community recreation halls or any meeting place that's available. Sunday mornings we could all come together. Once they have enough people, maybe they could come only once a month."

"Sounds really good," Julie said. Her eyes sparkled with enthusiasm. "Not only would we be saturating our community with the gospel but we would be able to monitor our upcoming pastors."

"That's right Julie," I said. "We can help them work out possible weak areas before sending them out to another city or country."

I met with the leadership to iron out the details, which we did. We began sending out teams of ten to fifteen people to different areas. We made sure that the team had music and that the others on the team were tithers to help with the expenses of printing literature, teaching supplies, and other needed materials.

When we sent out some of our best leaders and tithers, one of the brothers asked, "Pastor Sonny, won't sending out some of our faithful tithing people affect us at the parent church?"

"I really don't know," I responded. "But we will all know in a few weeks."

Once the satellite churches were in progress, the leadership met to evaluate what was happening. Surprisingly, as we released our very best leadership to reach our surrounding communities, it did not affect our finances. Every time we sent a group out, the Lord would replace them. The more we gave, the more we received.

We decided to meet with the satellite pastors once a week for encouragement and training. Julie also met periodically with the pastor's wives.

Once the churches were being established many of the young, zealous evangelists asked to meet with me.

Heading up the group was Johnnie Doss.

"Pastor Sonny, these churches are going to need people with the gift of evangelism to help them reach their communities. We want to be trained as satellite evangelists."

"That sounds great!" I said.

The plan was beautiful. These young men began having revivals and street rallies in the different areas. I was thrilled that they were getting "on the job" experience. One young man by the name of Joey was extremely effective in reaching the youth involved in gangs. He began "Teen Nite Satellites" in different areas and had great success.

My goal is to have these churches mushroom all over the city of Los Angeles. Eventually, as they mature, we will launch them into every major city in the United States and then the entire world.

This vision is not mine alone. But as the third and fourth generation churches continue to expand — inner city revival is eminent. We have learned and experienced in these past twenty years that God is still looking for faithful people who will believe Him for the impossible.

For example:

In the past few years the Lord has helped us penetrate into the prisons as never before. A revival among the vilest of sinners has been breaking out.

Prominent leaders of the Mexican mafia, the Aryan

Brotherhood, and many of the notorious prison gangs have given their lives to Christ. Former hit men and cold-blooded killers are being saved.

The Lord is unfolding His promise given to us years before in Isaiah: "And I will break down the gates of brass and cut asunder the bars of iron..."

Once such person is Art Blajos. While in prison he had an encounter with Christ and was saved. He spent seventeen cumulative years in prison, and fifteen of them were as an active member of the Mexican mafia.

For most of his life, he was surrounded by concrete and steel. He became what he calls, "inhuman." He was an assassin — a cold-blooded killer for the mafia. People were no more than targets to be executed. Art was a brutal animal with a total disregard for life. When he was released from prison, Art went into one of our Victory Outreach rehabilitation homes and totally committed his life to Jesus Christ.

Today, he is one of the young men that I have under my wing in intense discipleship. I can see him rising up and becoming a powerful asset to the ministry.

One of the most difficult sacrifices that Julie and I have ever made for the Lord were our children. God honored that and today one of the richest blessings of God is our children. Although they sacrificed in the earlier years, the Lord has used those experiences for good in their lives today. We have been very fortunate and blessed, because our children have grown to love God.

When they were younger they went through a period of being ashamed that I was a pastor to the outcasts of society. However, as they got older they began to appreciate and understand my calling.

Debbie, my oldest, graduated from Azusa Pacific University with a B.A. in telecommunications.

Doreen married Damon, a young man who graduated from our rehabilitation program and is expecting her second child. Doreen and Damon love the Lord and are very active in different areas of the ministry.

Georgina just graduated from high school and has plans to further her education.

Timothy is a senior in high school and is very active in sports.

Sonny Boy recently had a dynamic experience with Christ and has felt a call into full-time ministry. It wasn't always like that with him. As a parent, you wish your children would never leave God, and if they do, it breaks your heart.

Sonny Boy had been giving us a hard time. He had turned away from the Lord and began to drink, and one Saturday night, he went out to party. He openly chose to go his own way, it was one of the most difficult trials, as a parent, imaginable.

Sonny Boy arrived home at three in the morning. He tried to sneak in the house but the squeaky door gave him away. Julie had been waiting up for him and came downstairs. He played it cool, but she immediately noticed something was wrong and asked, "Where have you been?"

"I just went out with my friends to a restaurant," Sonny Boy responded. He continued to lie and make excuses. He didn't want to admit he'd been drinking.

"Come over here into the light," Julie said. Sonny Boy stepped into the light. "Let me smell your breath," she said sternly.

"No!" he said.

Again Julie said, "Let me smell your breath."

"No! What for?" he asked.

"Just let me smell your breath!" Julie was getting really upset.

Sonny Boy was intoxicated and defiantly stepped up to Julie and went, "Haa!" breathing right in her face. Julie slapped him in the face.

It was an instant reflex.

When she slapped him, tears rushed to her eyes. She looked at Sonny Boy and her tearful eyes showed the heartache she was feeling.

She came upstairs and crawled into my arms sobbing.

"What has happened to our son?" she cried. "What have we done wrong?"

She began blaming herself.

When Sonny Boy went into his room he could hear

his mother crying. This had a traumatic effect on him.

He started thinking, *What is wrong with me? What have I done? How far down am I going?*

The next day was Sunday.

During the morning service I saw Julie sitting with all of the family in the fourth row. I could see that she was under the strain of a sleepless night, coupled with the fear of possibly losing Sonny Boy to the deceit of the enemy.

Troubled with my thoughts I tried to preach. There were so many thoughts going through my mind that I stopped in the middle of the message and walked down off of the platform.

My head hung low as I painfully shared with the congregation: "Church, our family needs your prayers. Sonny, Timothy, Debbie, Doreen, Georgina, and Julie please come up here."

With heads bowed, they slowly walked up to the front of the church.

"The enemy wants to destroy my family," I continued, "and I will not permit this to happen! I want all of you to join me in fighting the spiritual warfare that has come against our family. Satan wants to destroy what Julie and I love most..." and I began to cry.

The congregation began to pray.

I could see that Sonny Boy was realizing how his wayward living was affecting us as a family. After that incident he seemed to get worse, but Julie and I, along with our church, joined forces in prayer for him. We were confident our Lord was going to do something in Sonny Boy's life.

A few months later Sonny Boy sat by himself in the back row of the church. At the close of the service I made the altar call and began to pray for the people who had come forward.

I was totally unaware that on the other side of the platform Sonny Boy was kneeling having responded to the call. As I prayed for each person I came to him — we locked eyes and for an instant I was awestruck. I looked over to Julie and could see her weeping .

I suddenly embraced Sonny Boy and began to weep and pray for him. "Thank You Jesus, my son, my son is here before You. Thank You,"

I sobbed. He also began to cry, as did the whole church. I could hear him whispering his repentance before God and this melted my heart — we stayed there for several minutes embracing, glorifying God for His faithfulness.

Sonny Boy experienced a genuine conversion and a true encounter with Christ.

At our prayer service some time later, he gave this stirring testimony:

> All my life, thus far, the enemy had me blinded. I was ashamed of my dad's ministry and the people he was called to minister to. I was embarrassed to bring home friends be-

cause some people that lived with us had a lot of tattoos and looked so rough and tough. Every time someone would ask me if drug addicts and prostitutes lived with us I would brush it off and stay away from the subject.

All of us kids resented giving up our beds so that people could come in to kick their habits. However, I want to declare something to you tonight.

I'm beginning to understand the urgency of my dad's mission and I now see things so differently. I am proud of you, Mom and Dad. Dad, I want you to know I want to grow and mature to be a man of God just like you.

As time went on Julie and I could tell that the Lord had separated our son and had chosen him to serve Him in full-time ministry, but this reality had to be branded by God in Sonny Boy's heart.

He expressed a desire to go to Amsterdam so he could establish within himself his own identity in Christ. He wanted to see where he fit in the whole picture of the vision. He said he didn't want to ride on my coat tails. Julie and I, respecting his decision, prayed and released him. Shortly after being in Amsterdam, we received this letter:

Dear Mom and Dad,

I'm writing to you from the basement here in the Amsterdam Victory Outreach Training Center. I miss you a lot. While I was praying, I wrote down a few things that I felt God dealing with me and speaking to my heart about.

I feel strongly that I should come to Amsterdam for a year, but I'm going to keep praying and make sure that it's what God really wants me to do. It's gonna take a lot of sacrifice.

But I know it will really develop me as a man of God. I think it will also let me find exactly what God has planned for my life. I love the Lord with all my heart. I want to accomplish His will for my life. I want to press toward the mark of His high calling on my life. I also want to be an example for my brothers and sisters: Debbie, Doreen, Georgina, and Timothy. They mean a lot to me; I want to see them going forward for God. I love them so much. I may not show it at times but I really do care about them and about their future.

But the bottom line is that I just want God's will for my life and I want His heart. At home there's a lot of pressures on me; not only that everyone thinks of me as Sonny, Jr. I'm proud to be your son, but I also want to be my own person that God moves through separately. I want to build something for God and really know that God has called me for myself. Love, Sonny

Sonny Boy stayed in Amsterdam for a year. When he came back he returned with a confirmation of his calling to the ministry.

He enrolled in Life Bible College and began preaching the Word with boldness.

One of the most rewarding and thrilling experiences Julie and I have ever experienced was when, in front of 10,000 people at Victory Outreach International 1991 Summer Conference, I was able to license and launch out my own son "Sonny Boy" as an official Victory Outreach evangelist.

I know the Lord has a great work ahead for "my special Treasure Out of Darkness."

Julie:

Kathy Clark, a long-time friend, had driven me to the Los Angeles City Morgue to interview the coroner, Dr. Noguchi. I needed to acquire statistics on "Death and Teenagers" for Sonny's television program.

It was a warm, sunny Wednesday afternoon. I had confronted many uncomfortable situations, but I was totally unprepared for what lay ahead for me in the morgue. As Kathy walked with me into the entrance of the autopsy room, the smell of death was staggering.

My cameraman hadn't arrived yet, but I felt that I

couldn't possibly do the interview there. I couldn't tolerate the smell.

"Julie, compose yourself. This will be over quickly. You need to get these facts. Let me pray for you," said Kathy.

"I made a mistake. I don't have the stomach for this." I looked around and saw an opened refrigerator. I could see the feet of a corpse. A nauseous feeling come over me.

"Come on Julie. You can do all things through Christ who strengthens you. Let me pray for you." Kathy began to pray. I began to feel a peace. She continued praying, "Lord, strengthen Julie and cover her with the blood of Jesus. We know that Your perfect love casts out all fear."

"Feel better now Julie?" she asked.

"Yes, and thank you for the prayer."

After making sure I was okay, she said good bye. Just as the door closed behind her, Dr. Noguchi walked in. "Hello, Dr. Noguchi," I said confidently. "My cameraman should be here any minute. Maybe we can take advantage of these few minutes to get acquainted?"

"Sure, Mrs. Arguinzoni."

"Call me Julie, please," I said.

I began to ask him questions about teenagers and death. He told me how a good percentage of those that end up in the city morgue died violent deaths such as suicides, murders, rapes, mutilations, and stabbings.

Many of them were teenage transients with no one to claim their bodies.

"How long do you keep the body?" I asked.

"We keep them for six months and if no one comes to claim them we dispose of the body," he answered.

"How do you dispose of it?" I asked.

"By cremation. Would you like to take a tour of the facilities?" he asked.

"Yes, please," I stammered. "I guess so."

Just as we walked out of the autopsy room, they were bringing in the body of a man who had just been shot while he was repossessing a car. He was a big fellow, weighing about 400 pounds. His body was still soft and looked as if he was only asleep. That was shocking to see.

"Now follow me this way," the doctor said.

I followed close behind him as we walked down the hallway, where there were bodies lining the walls waiting to be processed. I had never seen anything like that. The clerks who worked there were so accustomed to the smell and sight of death, that they were oblivious to their surroundings. Somehow, that disturbed me.

He then opened a refrigerator door and asked me to enter first. I walked in and was shocked to see the bodies stacked up three tiers high. They were placed on steel slabs — two to three on a slab. Jane Doe, John Doe. Over and over again I read the same names on tags tied to their toes.

"Who are these people," I asked, "and why are they here?"

We continued walking. I kept staring at the tags, Jane Doe, John Doe.

"These are the bodies that we keep for six months."

"How many are here?" I stammered.

"There are 350 in this refrigerator and the one next door has another 250."

I suddenly started shaking and had a horrible, frightening feeling.

I then heard a voice as if it were laughing in my face, "This is my trophy room."

I immediately recognized who it was.

He repeated, "This is my trophy room."

At first fear gripped me.

I wanted to run as I thought, *Oh God, I'm here in Satan's trophy room. These people have died in horrendous ways and this is his display.*

The Lord then reassured me, "Julie, you don't have to run from the enemy. This might be his trophy room, but you come back at him. You have My power within you!"

I knew that after the Crucifixion and Resurrection, Jesus sent His church the power of the Holy Spirit.

Hebrews 2:14 and 15 says, "...that by his death he might destroy him who holds the power of death — that is, the devil — and free those who all their lives were held in slavery by their fear of death."

I could almost hear Satan snarling at me. Instead of running, a Holy Ghost boldness came over me and I screamed out at him, "Satan, this might be your trophy room, but God has promised us 'Treasures Out of Darkness.' This may be your trophy room, your treasures, and it may be too late for them; but we're going to win tens of thousands out of your clutches. We have just begun to give you a battle. Sonny and I, and all of the trophies God has given us, are going to continue to fight you; with the Lord Jesus on our side, the war is won!"

I left the morgue trembling and crying. I called Sonny on the phone and told him about the experience that I had and of how the enemy had spoken to me so clearly.

"Sonny," I cried, "we're in a battle over people's souls and we've got to continue to 'fight the fight of faith' for God. We must continue to win souls all over the world. Let's believe God for millions of Treasures Out of Darkness!"

Today we have over one hundred rehabilitation sites and have planted over one hundred churches. We have established national and international ministries: United Women in Ministry, Victory Outreach School of Ministry, Youth With a Vision, a television ministry, and much more.

This is just the beginning!

There are millions upon millions whose names are written in the Lamb's Book of Life because they have believed in Jesus, the Son of God. They will enjoy an eternity with Christ, walking on streets paved with gold ... There will be no sickness, no tears, and no condemnation.

Satan may have his trophy rooms where his followers are guaranteed an eternity of torment and a burning hell, but the Lord continues daily to add thousands upon thousands of treasures who have come out of darkness and are today redeemed and guaranteed an eternity of joy and reward:

Sonny & Julie Arguinzoni, Debora, Sonny Boy, Georgina, and Timothy Arguinzoni; Doreen and Damon Kuklinski; Gibert and Mary Garavito; Rudy Hernandez; Saul and Stella Garcia; Kathy Clark; Doug Hollis; David and Donna Diaz, New York City; Nolberto and Marilyn Gomez, Barcelona, Spain; Maria Jesus, Spain; Steve and Joesy Pineda; Mando and Arline; Pepe, Ed and Mitzi; Raul and Gina Diaz, Amsterdam, Holland; Philip and Cindy; Koumebio and Charity Komlan, West Africa; Julian and Soraya, São Paulo, Brazil; Art Blajos; Helen Jackson; Robert and Delores; Al Apodaca, Honolulu; Ray and Sylvia; Juan Escamilla; Rubin and Mary; Carlos and Frances, Mexico; Donny and Yvonne; Brian and Vivian, Londan, England; Richard and Salina Ledesma, Hawaii; Joe and Tina Lugo; Ray and Sylvia Chavez; Anthony and Diana Ponce; David and Faith Martinez; Tony and Nellie Guzman, San Diego; Rick and Jeannie Alanis